*The*

# NEW ENGLAND ECONOMICAL HOUSEKEEPER,

## AND FAMILY RECEIPT BOOK.

This facsimile edition of *The New England Economical Housekeeper, and Family Receipt Book* by Esther A. Howland was reproduced by permission from the volume in the collection of the American Antiquarian Society (AAS), Worcester, Massachusetts. Founded in 1812 by Isaiah Thomas, a Revolutionary War patriot and successful printer and publisher, the Society is a research library documenting the life of Americans from the colonial era through 1876. AAS aims to collect, preserve, and make available as complete a record as possible of the printed materials from the early American experience. The cookbook collection includes approximately 1,100 volumes.

Esther Howland wrote her recipe book of regional New England cookery for those "who would cook well at a moderate expense." *The New England Economical Housekeeper, and Family Receipt Book*, published in Worcester, Massachusetts, in 1844, emphasized household economy and frugality—important themes in nineteenth century home management as the middle class expanded and redefined the domestic ideals of American society.

*The*

# NEW ENGLAND ECONOMICAL HOUSEKEEPER,

## AND FAMILY RECEIPT BOOK.

ESTHER A. HOWLAND

INTRODUCTION BY BARBARA LYNCH

**Andrews McMeel**
**Publishing, LLC**
Kansas City • Sydney • London

Andrews McMeel Publishing, LLC
an Andrews McMeel Universal company
1130 Walnut Street, Kansas City, Missouri 64106

www.andrewsmcmeel.com

13 14 15 16 17 POA 10 9 8 7 6 5 4 3 2 1

ISBN: 978-1-4494-3174-7

Library of Congress Control Number: 2013930719

ATTENTION: SCHOOLS AND BUSINESSES
Andrews McMeel books are available at quantity discounts with bulk purchase for educational, business, or sales promotional use. For information, please e-mail the Andrews McMeel Publishing Special Sales Department: specialsales@amuniversal.com

# INTRODUCTION
## *by* BARBARA LYNCH

While I've spent the majority of my career as a chef focused on French and Italian cuisine, I grew up in South Boston the second-youngest of seven children with a mother who found ways to creatively stretch a dollar to feed her large family. I don't think my mother particularly enjoyed cooking and certainly didn't forage for ingredients or spend time baking from scratch, but the spirit of doing a lot with a little was certainly alive and well. Mrs. Esther Howland captures this thrifty Yankee spirit in a book that, though originally published in 1844, proves to be way ahead of its time. Esther offers a complete resource for housekeepers that includes not just clear and concise recipes, but sections dedicated to the myriad other challenges that arise when caring for a household—ranging from treating burns and chapped hands to how to fatten fowls, remove flies from rooms, and fashion fire escapes. Long before the plethora of housekeeping magazines and newspapers (and much later, the Internet) of today were available, this book surely must have been a go-to for advice and how-to tips.

After many years cooking in professional kitchens and spending time learning about French and Italian culinary traditions, I discovered a similar practical spirit that has certainly come back in style among those interested in food, nutrition, and the environment. In recent years, a renewed interest in where food comes from, a "do it yourself" movement, and a challenging economy have meant that people are getting back into the kitchen and becoming more resourceful. Passion and necessity have fueled everything from urban foraging to bread baking and jam making to a rising popularity in "home remedies."

Reading this book, I was endlessly fascinated by the recipes—an impressive collection of New England classics that includes a number of puddings as well as breads, biscuits, cakes, soups, roasts, and more—and found myself researching countless ingredients including saleratus (now known as baking soda), sago, and Havana sugar, and being inspired to make my own vinegar and potato starch. While no recipe is overly complex, admirable attention is given to the importance of proper technique, and the dishes strike a balance between good taste and frugality. The preface notes that for the recipes shared, the book "is particularly recommended to the attention of those who would cook well, at a moderate expense," which is evident in the lengthy direction given for boiling meats: "This may give rather more trouble, but those who wish to excel in their art must only consider how the processes of it can be most perfectly performed; a cook who has a proper pride and pleasure in her business, will make this her maxim on all occasions." As a chef, I appreciate the respect and dignity ascribed to the craft of cooking and the recognition that food is more than sustenance—it is a pleasure and an art (at any price point!).

*The Economical New England Housekeeper* is not only a glimpse back at the way life used to be but a reminder of the possibility that one may run a household wisely, creatively, and deliciously on a budget. And today, that thrifty, "can-do" Yankee spirit will most certainly serve everyone well.

〜✴〜

James Beard Award-winner Chef Barbara Lynch is regarded as one of Boston's—and the country's—leading chefs and restaurateurs. As founder and CEO of Barbara Lynch Gruppo, she oversees eight celebrated culinary concepts in Boston: No.9 Park, B&G Oysters, The Butcher Shop, Stir, Drink, Sportello, 9 at Home, and Menton, Boston's only Relais & Chateaux property. Barbara and her recipes have been featured in many publications, including *Saveur, Boston Common, Bon Appétit*, the *New York Times*, and *Inc.* magazine. Her television appearances include *Top Chef, Today*, and as a judge on The Food Network; and she is the subject of a documentary film entitled *Amuse Bouche—A Chef's Tale*.

In 2011, she was named Distinguished Chef by Johnson and Wales University. She is also a member of notable industry organizations including Women Chefs & Restaurateurs and Maîtres Cuisiniers, the international association of Master Chefs. In 2011, Women Chefs & Restaurateurs presented her with the Barbara Tropp President's Award and in 2013, Barbara was inducted into the James Beard Foundation's Who's Who of Food and Beverage in America, a prestigious group of the most accomplished food and beverage professionals in the country, and also received an honorary doctorate in public service from Northeastern University in recognition of her culinary and philanthropic contributions. As a member of the Bocuse d'Or USA Culinary Council, Barbara judged the Bocuse d'Or Commis and Finalist Competition in 2012. Because of her unique story and entrepreneurial insight, Barbara has had the privilege of participating as a panelist and speaker at events including The Ad Club's Women in Leadership Forum, the Massachusetts Conference for Women, and Women Chefs & Restaurateurs' National Conference.

THE

# NEW ENGLAND

# ECONOMICAL HOUSEKEEPER,

AND

# FAMILY RECEIPT BOOK.

[ Mrs. E. A. Howland ]

———◆———

WORCESTER:
PUBLISHED BY S. A. HOWLAND.
1844.

JONATHAN L. ESTEY, PRINTER,
At the Ægis Office, Worcester.

# PREFACE.

—

This work has been compiled with a careful regard to the most economical mode of preparing the various dishes for which directions have been given; and is particularly recommended to the attention of those who would cook well, at a moderate expense. Many of the receipts are new, having been prepared, or furnished, expressly for this work. Selections have also been made from various works on this subject, such as have been proved to be good by use.

The Medicinal Department will be found to contain a select number of useful and tried remedies, for the various ills and accidents that occur in almost every family; although not intended as a substitute for the family physician, still, there are times when his attendance or advice cannot be had at the moment when most needed; it is then, that the receipts in this Department will be found to be of some service.

In conclusion, we would tender our thanks to those friends who have kindly furnished some of their choice and valuable receipts; and to those into whose hands our little work may come, we would bespeak a fair trial before passing judgment against it.

# CONTENTS.

# CONTENTS.

## MEDICINAL DEPARTMENT.

## WEIGHT AND MEASURE.

Wheat Flour, one pound is one quart.

Indian Meal, one pound two ounces is one quart.

Butter, when soft, one pound is one quart.

White Sugar powdered, one pound one ounce is one quart.

Best Brown Sugar, one pound two ounces is one quart.

## LIQUIDS.

Sixteen large table-spoonfuls are half a pint.

Eight do. do. do. are one gill.

Four do. do. do. are half a gill.

Twenty-five drops are equal to one tea-spoonful.

A common wine glass to half a gill.

A common tumbler to half a pint.

# THE ECONOMICAL HOUSEKEEPER.

### 1. Ripe Bread.

Bread made of wheat flour when taken out of the oven is unprepared for the stomach. It should go through a change or ripen before it is eaten. Young persons, or persons in the enjoyment of vigorous health, may eat bread immediately after being baked without any sensible injury from it, but weakly and aged persons cannot, and none can eat such without doing harm to the digestive organs. Bread after being baked goes through a change similar to the change in newly brewed beer, or newly churned butter-milk, neither being healthy until after the change. During the change in bread it sends off a large portion of *carbon*, or unhealthy gas, and imbibes a large portion of *oxygen*, or healthy gas. Bread has according to the computation of physicians, one fifth more nutriment in it when ripe, than it has when just out of the oven. It not only has more nutriment but imparts a much greater degree of cheerfulness. He that eats old ripe bread will have a much greater flow of animal spirits than he would were he to eat unripe bread. Bread, as before observed, discharges carbon and imbibes oxygen. One thing in connection with this thought should be particularly noticed by all housewives. It is, to let the bread ripen where it can inhale the oxygen in a pure state. Bread will always taste of the air that surrounds it while ripening — hence it should ripen where the air is pure. It should never ripen in a cellar, nor in a close cupboard, nor in a bed-room. The noxious vapors of a cellar, or a cupboard, never should enter into and form a

2

part of the bread we eat. Bread should be *light, well baked, and properly ripened,* before it should be eaten.

Bread that is several days old, may be renewed so as to have all the freshness and lightness of new bread, by simply putting it into a common steamer over a fire, and steaming it half or three quarters of an hour. The vessel under the steamer containing the water, should not be more than half full, otherwise the water may boil up into the steamer and wet the bread. After the bread is thus steamed, it should be taken out of the steamer, and wrapped loosely in a cloth to dry and cool, and remain so two or three hours, when it will be ready to be cut and used. It will then be like cold new bread.

### 2. Cheap, Light, and Wholesome Bread.

Take a dozen and a half of good mealy potatoes well boiled ; peel them and mash them fine while warm ; add two quarts of cold water and then strain the mixture through a cullender ; add flour enough to make a thick batter ; then a pint of good lively yeast or emptyings ; if the yeast is sweet, no saleratus is necessary ; if sour a very little saleratus ; let the sponge set until it is well fermented. With this sponge you may make a large or a small quantity of bread by adding flour and water or milk ; if a small quantity, it may be put into the oven very soon ; if the quantity be large it must stand longer, or over night. Put in double the usual quantity of salt, but no shortening. Let the dough stand in a place moderately warm, but not near the fire, unless it is to be baked immediately. Milk or water may be used, but water is the best, for the sponge mixed with water keeps sweet the longest. The bread will be very light, sweet, and wholesome, having in it neither acids nor alkalies to neutralize each other. The greater the proportion of potatoes the lighter the bread will be ; but if the proportion is very large the bread will be so light as to dry up if kept several days.

### 3. Another.

Six ounces of bran boiled one hour and a half in five pints of water ; strain the liquid from the bran, and dilute it with water sufficient to make the bread. Two ounces of salt : five pounds of good flour : two table spoons full of yeast. In baking a large quantity, each article must be proportionably increased.

### 4. Brown Bread.

Put the Indian meal in your bread pan, sprinkle a little salt among it, and wet it thoroughly with scalding water. When it is cool, put in your rye ; add two gills of lively yeast, and mix it with water as stiff as you can knead it. Let it stand an hour and a half, in a cool place in summer, on the hearth in winter. It should be put into a very hot oven, and baked three or four hours.

### 5. Dyspepsia Bread.

Three quarts unbolted wheat meal ; one quart soft water, warm, but not hot ; one gill of fresh yeast ; one gill of molasses, or not, as may suit the taste ; one tea spoonful of saleratus.

### 6. To make Rice Bread.

Boil a pint of rice soft; add a pint of leaven ; then, three quarts of the flour : put it to rise in a tin or earthen vessel until it has risen sufficiently ; divide it into three parts; then bake it as other bread, and you will have three large loaves.

### 7. Wisconsin Loaf Bread.

Stir Indian meal in skim milk to the consistency of pan-cake batter, about two quarts. Add two tea-spoonfuls of molasses, one of saleratus, two of shortening, and two tea-cups of wheat flour. Stir in the evening, bake in the morning, and eat while hot.

### 8. Sponge Bread.

Make a batter of flour and water, thickness of flat jacks, put it in a tin pail, and sit this pail in a kettle of warm water, five or six hours, till it has risen ; then mould it hard by adding more flour, and make it into loaves in basins, and let it stand till it begins to crack open ; it is now ready to be put into the oven and will bake in from thirty to forty-five minutes.

### 9. Cream Tartar Bread.

One quart flour, two tea-spoonfuls of cream tartar, one of saleratus, two and a half cups milk, bake 20 minutes.

### 10. Yeast Bread.

Three pints of milk or water to one cup full of yeast, stir in flour enough to make it a little thicker than flat jacks rise it over night, mould it up and let it stand till it rises, then bake it.

### 11. Brown Bread made of Indian and Wheat Meal.

Take one quart of Indian meal, and one quart of wheat meal, one quart of sour milk, half tea-cupful molasses, heaping tea-spoonful saleratus, and a little salt, stir it with a spoon, and bake it, in a tin or iron basin, about two hours.

### 12. Another -- Rye and Indian.

Take about two quarts of Indian meal and scald it, then add as much rye meal, a teacup full of molasses half a pint of lively yeast; if the yeast is sweet, no saleratus is necessary; if sour, put in a little, let it stand from one to two hours, till it rises, then bake it about three hours.

### 13. Rolls.

Warm an ounce of butter in half a pint of milk, then add a spoonful and a half of yeast. and a little salt. Put two pounds of flour in a pan, and mix in the above ingredients. Let it rise an hour—or over night in a cool place; knead it well, make into seven rolls, and bake them in a quick oven. Add half a tea-spoonful of saleratus just as you put the rolls into the baker.

### 14. Short Rolls.

Take about two pounds of flour, add a piece of butter half the size of an egg, a little salt, an egg, two spoonsful of yeast, and mix it with warm milk, make it into a light dough, and let it stand by the fire all night; should it sour, put in a little saleratus. Bake them in a quick oven.

### 15. Sour Milk Biscuit.

Have ready your flour, sweeten your milk with a little saleratus, add a little salt, make it rather soft, and pour it into your pan and bake it.

### 16. Brown Bread Biscuit.

Two quarts of Indian meal, a pint and a half of rye, one cup of flour, two spoonsful of yeast, and a table

spoonful of molasses. It is well to add a little saleratus
to yeast almost always, just as you put it into the article.
Let it rise over night.

### 17. Bread Biscuit.

Three pounds of flour, half a pint of Indian meal sifted, a little butter, two spoonfuls of lively yeast; set it
before the fire to rise over night; mix it with warm
water.

### 18. Newton Biscuits.

Make a pound of flour, the yolk of an egg, and some
milk into a very stiff paste; beat it well, knead it till
smooth, roll it thin and cut it into biscuits; prick, and
bake them in a slow oven till dry and crisp.

### 19. Light Biscuit.

Take two pounds of flour, a pint of buttermilk, half
a tea-spoonful of saleratus, put into the buttermilk a
small piece of butter or lard rubbed into the flour;
make it about the consistency of bread before baking.

### 20. Rice Biscuit.

Two pounds of flour, a tea-cupful of rice, well boiled,
two spoonsful of yeast, mix it with warm water: and let
it rise six or eight hours.

### 21. Griddle Cakes.

Rub three ounces of butter into a pound of flour with
a little salt, moisten it with sweet buttermilk to make it
into paste, roll it out and cut the cakes with the cover
of your dredging box, and put them upon a griddle to
bake.

### 22. Rolls, American.

Three pints of sifted flour, six spoonfuls of yeast, a
pint of lukewarm water, a tea-spoonful of salt, half a
pint more of warm water, and a little more flour mixed
in before kneading.

### 23. Superior Johnny-Cake.

Take one quart of milk, three eggs, one tea-spoonful
saleratus, one tea-cup of wheat flour, and Indian meal
sufficient to make a batter of the consistency of pan-
cakes. Bake quick, in pans previously buttered, and

2*

eat warm with butter or milk. The addition of wheat flour will be found to be a great improvement in the art of making these cakes.

### 24. Milk Biscuit.

Two pounds of sifted flour, eight ounces butter, two eggs, three gills milk, a gill and a half yeast. Cut the butter into the milk and warm it slightly, sift the flour into a pan and pour the milk and butter into it. Beat the eggs and pour them in also, lastly the yeast; mix all well together with a knife. Flour your moulding board, put the lump of dough on it and knead it very hard. Then cut the dough in small pieces and knead them into round balls, prick and set them in buttered pans to rise till light, probably about an hour, and bake in a moderate oven.

### 25. Butter Biscuit.

Eight ounces butter, two pounds flour sifted, half pint milk or cold water, a salt-spoonful of salt. Cut up the butter in the flour and put the salt to it, wet it to a stiff dough with the milk or water, mix it well with a knife. Throw some flour on the moulding board, take the dough out of the pan and knead it very well. Roll it out into a large thick sheet and beat it very hard on both sides with the rolling pin. Beat it a long time, cut it out with a tin or cup, into small round thick cakes. Beat each cake on both sides with the rolling pin, prick them with a fork, put them in buttered pans and bake them of a light brown in a slow oven.

### 26. Yeast.

To have good yeast in summer, is a desirable object with every housewife. She may have such by the following simple process :

Boil a single handful of hops (which every farmer can and ought to raise, to the extent of household wants,) in two or three quarts of water — strain and thicken the liquor, when hot, with rye flour; then add two or three small yeast or turnpike cakes, to set the mass. If this is done at evening it will be fit for use early next morning. Reserve a pint of this yeast, which thicken with Indian meal, make into small cakes, the size of crackers, and dry them in the shade for future use. In this

way the yeast is always fresh and active. Yeast cakes
kept a long time are apt to become rancid, and lose their
virtues. The fresher the cakes the better the yeast.

### 27. Another.

Boil one pound of good flour and a quarter of a
pound of brown sugar, and a little salt, in two gallons of water for one hour. When milk warm, bottle it
and cork it close, and it will be fit for use in twenty-four
hours. One pint of the yeast will make 18 lbs. of bread.

### 28. To preserve Bread, or prevent it from moulding.

Bread that is kept in a damp place, or not used soon
after a heavy rain, is apt to collect a kind of moss or
mould. This can be easily prevented by mixing a small
quantity of arrow root with wheaten flour, before the
dough is ready for the oven. It is also useful in preparing sea biscuit for long voyages.

### 29. Cup Cake.

One cup butter, two cups sugar, three cups flour, and
four eggs, well beat together, and baked twenty minutes,
in pans or cups.

### 30. Election Cake.

Four pounds flour; three fourths pound butter; four
eggs; one pound sugar; half pint good yeast; wet it
with milk as soft as can be moulded on a board. Set to
rise over night in winter; in warm weather, three hours
is usually enough for it to rise. Bake about three fourths
of an hour.

### 31. Sponge Cake.

The weight of six eggs in sugar, the weight of four
eggs in flour, a little rose-water. The whites and yolks
should be beaten thoroughly and separately. The eggs
and sugar should be well beaten together; but after
the flour is sprinkled, it should not be stirred a moment
longer than is necessary to mix it well; it should be
poured into the pan, and got into the oven with all possible expedition. Twenty minutes is about long enough
to bake.

### 32. Another.

Four large eggs, two cups flour, two cups sugar—even
full; beat the two parts of the eggs separate, the white

to a froth, then beat them together, then stir in the flour and without delay put into the oven.

### 33. Cheap Sponge Cake.

Four eggs, three cups sugar, one cup milk, teaspoonful saleratus, flour enough to make it a good stiff batter, a little salt and spice,—quick oven.   Bake 20 minutes.

### 34. Loaf Cake.

Two pounds flour, half pound sugar, quarter pound butter, two eggs, a gill of sweet emptyings, half ounce cinnamon, or cloves, a large spoonful rose-water ; if it is not about as thin as good white bread dough, add a little milk.   Bake about three fourths of an hour.

### 35. Caraway Cakes.

Take one pound flour, 3-4ths lb. sugar, half lb. butter, a glass rose-water, four eggs, and half a teacup caraway seed,—the materials well rubbed together and beat up. Drop them from a spoon on tin sheets, and bake them twenty or thirty minutes in rather a slow oven.

### 36. Short Cake.

Rub in a very small bit of shortening, or three tablespoonfuls cream, with the flour ; put in a tea-spoonful strong dissolved saleratus, into your sour milk, and mix the cake pretty stiff, to bake in a spider on a few embers.

### 37. Wedding Cake.

Four pounds flour, three pounds butter, three pounds sugar, four pounds currants, two pounds raisins, twenty-four eggs, one ounce mace, and three nutmegs.   A little molasses makes it dark colored, which is desirable.— Half a pound of citron improves it.   Bake two and a half or three hours.

### 38. Another.

Four pounds flour, three lbs. butter, four lbs. sugar, thirty eggs, three and a half lbs. currants, one lb. citron, one ounce mace, a little cinnamon, very little cloves, make into loaves of convenient size.   Bake two and a half or three hours.

### 39. Frosting for Cake.

Beat the whites of eggs to an entire froth, and to each egg add five tea-spoonfuls sifted loaf sugar, gradually; beat it a great while. Put it on when your cake is hot, or cold, as is most convenient. A little lemon juice squeezed into the egg and sugar, improves it. Spread it on with a knife, and smooth it over with a soft brush, like a shaving brush.

#### 40. Cheap Tea Cake.

Three cups of sugar, three eggs, one cup of butter, one cup of milk, a spoonful of dissolved saleratus, and four cups of flour well beat up. If it is so stiff it will not stir easily add a little more milk.

#### 41. Gingerbread.

Rub four and a half pounds of flour with half a pound of lard and half a pound of butter; a pint of molasses, a gill of milk, tea-cup of ginger, a tea-spoonful of saleratus, stirred together. All mixed, baked in shallow pans, twenty or thirty minutes.

#### 42. Soft Gingerbread.

Six tea cups of flour, three of molasses, one of cream, one of butter, one table-spoonful of ginger, and one of saleratus.

#### 43. Sugar Gingerbread.

Nine eggs, two pounds flour, one and a half of sugar, one cup ginger, one glass rosewater. Make it very thin and sift sugar over it as you put it in the oven.

#### 44. Family Gingerbread.

Four cups molasses, two cups boiling water, four tea-spoonfuls saleratus, small piece melted butter, make it stiff with flour, roll it thin, bake in pans.

#### 45. Composition Cake.

One pound of flour, one of sugar, half a pound of butter, seven eggs, and half a pint of cream.

#### 46. Tea Cake.

Three cups of sugar, three eggs, one cup of butter, one cup of milk, two cups of flour, a small lump of saleratus and make it not quite as stiff as pound cake.

#### 47. Loaf Cake.

Five pounds of flour, two of sugar, three quarters of a pound of lard, and the same quantity of butter, one pint of yeast, eight eggs, one quart of milk ; roll the sugar into the flour ; add the raisins and spice after the first rising.

### 48. Wafers.

One pound of flour, quarter of a pound of butter, two eggs beat, one glass of quince preserve juice and a nutmeg.

### 49. Jumbles.

Three pounds of flour, two of sugar, one of butter, eight eggs, with a little caraway seed ; and a little milk if the eggs are not sufficient.

### 50. Soft Cakes in little pans.

One and a half pound of butter rubbed into two pounds of flour, add one wine glass of preserve juice, one of rose-water, two of yeast, nutmeg, cinnamon, and currants.

### 51. Sponge Cake.

Five eggs, half a pound of sugar, and a quarter of a poundof flour.

### 52. Pound Cake.

Three eggs, nine spoonfuls of butter, three of sugar, and three handfuls of flour.

### 53. Shrewsbury Cake.

One pound of flour, three quarters of a pound of sugar, three quarters of a pound of butter, four eggs, one nutmeg.

### 54. Clove Cake.

Three pounds of flour, one of butter, one of sugar, three eggs, two spoonfuls of cloves — mix it with molosses.

### 55. Wonders.

Two pounds of flour, three quarters of a pounds of sugar, half a pound of butter, nine eggs, a little mace and rose water.

### 56. Indian Flat Jacks.

Scald a quart of Indian meal, when lukewarm stir in half a pint of flour, half a tea cup full of yeast and a little salt when light, fry them in just fat enough to prevent their sticking to the pan.

### 57. Indian Griddle Cakes, or Flat Jacks.

One pint Indian meal, one cup flour, a little salt and ginger, a table-spoonful molasses, a tea-spoonful saleratus, sour milk enough to make a stiff batter. Bake or fry them on a griddle, or in a spider, like buck-wheat cakes.

### 58. Rice Flat Jacks.

Boil some rice thin; add a pint of sour milk, then thicken with flour, add a little salt and saleratus.

### 59. Common Flat Jacks.

One quart sour milk, thicken with flour, two tea-spoonfuls saleratus, and a little salt.

### 60. Pancakes.

Half a pint of milk, three spoonfuls of sugar, one or two eggs, a tea-spoonful of dissolved saleratus, spiced with cinnamon, or cloves, a little salt, and rose-water. Flour should be stirred in till the spoon moves around with difficulty. Have the fat in your skillet boiling hot, and drop them in with a spoon; and cook till thoroughly brown.

### 61. Nut Cakes.

One pound of flour, quarter of a pound of butter, quarter of a pound of sugar, five eggs, spice.

### 62. Plain Cake.

Three pounds flour, one of sugar, one of butter, half pint yeast, three gills milk, three eggs, spice, rose-water.

### 63. Plum Cake.

Mix together a pint of lukewarm milk, two quarts of sifted flour, a small tea-cup of yeast. Set it where it will rise quick. When quite light work in with the hand four beaten eggs, a tea-spoonful of salt, two of cinnamon. Stir a pound of sugar with three quarters of a pound of butter; when white, work it into the cake, add another quart of sifted flour, and beat the whole ten or fifteen minutes and set it where it will rise again ; when of a spongy lightness, put it into buttered cake pans and let them stand fifteen or twenty minutes before baking. Add, if you like, a pound and a half of raisins, just before putting the cake in the pans.

### 64. Cream Cake.

Sift some double refined sugar, beat the whites of seven or eight eggs; shake in as many spoonfuls of the sugar, grate in the rind of a large lemon, drop the froth on a paper, laid on tin, in lumps at a distance; sift a good deal of sugar over them, set them in a moderate oven. The froth will rise — put them in a cool oven to dry. You may put raspberry jam and put two bottoms together.

### 65. Another and better.

Six eggs, seven cups sugar, twelve cups flour, one pint cream, one tea-spoonful saleratus, — salt, spice and plums, to suit your taste; bake from one and a half, to two hours.

### 66. Cookies.

Five cups flour, two of sugar, one of butter, one egg, one tea-spoonful of saleratus, and cut it with a tin into small cakes.

### 67. Another.

One cup butter, well mixed with two and half cups, sugar, three eggs, one cup milk, one tea-spoonful saleratus, salt and spice to your taste, flour enough to mould it.

### 68. New Year's Cake.

A very good and plain cake can be made without eggs. Take seven pounds of flour, two and a half pounds of sugar, two pounds of butter, one pint of water and two tea-spoonfuls of saleratus well dissolved. Roll it out thin, and bake it on tin sheets. It will keep good a long time.

### 69. Buns.

Rub four ounces of butter into two pounds of flour, four ounces of sugar, and a few caraway seeds if you like them. Put a spoonful or two of cream into a cup of yeast, and as much good milk as will make the above into a light paste — set it to rise, bake it on tins before a quick fire.

### 70. Seed Cakes.

One tea-cup of butter, two cups sugar rubbed into four cups flour; mix with milk hard enough to roll, half a tea-spoonful of saleratus, seeds to your taste.

### 71. Another.

Four cups flour, one and a half cream or milk, half cup butter, three eggs, two cups sugar, tea-spoonful saleratus, half cup seeds, rose water.

### 72. Loaf Cake.

Two pounds sifted flour, setting aside half a pound of it to sprinkle in at the last, one pound fresh butter, one pound of powdered sugar, four eggs, one pound of raisins stoned and cut in half, one pound currants (imported) washed and dried, half pint milk, some preserve juice or lemon peel grated, a table-spoonful of mace, cinnamon and nutmeg mixed, half a pint of the best yeast or more if it is not very strong. Cut up the butter in the milk and warm it till the butter is quite soft, then stir it together and set it away to cool, it must not be made too warm. After you have beaten the eggs, mix them with the butter and milk, and stir the whole into the pan of flour. Add the spice and liquor and stir in the sugar gradually. Having poured off the thin from the top, stir the yeast and pour it into the mixture, then sprinkle in the rest of the flour. Have ready the fruit, which must be well floured, stir it gradually into the mixture, butter a large tin pan and put the cake into it, cover it and set it in a warm place five or six hours to rise ; when quite light bake in a moderate oven.

### 73. Cheap Loaf Cake.

Two cups flour, one cup molasses, two eggs well beat up, half cup currants, half cup raisins, half tea-spoonful cloves, half do. nutmegs, one do. saleratus, half cup butter.

### 74. Cup Cake.

Five eggs, two large tea-cupfuls molasses, same of brown sugar rolled fine, same of fresh butter, one cup rich milk, five cups flour sifted ; add powdered allspice, cloves, and ginger, to your liking. Cut up the butter in the milk, warm them slightly, warm also the molasses and stir it into the milk and butter, then stir in gradually the sugar and let it cool. Beat the eggs very light and stir them into the mixture alternately with the flour, add the ginger and other spice and stir the whole very hard. Butter small tins, nearly fill them with the mixture, and bake the cakes in a moderate oven.

### 75. Temperance Cake.

Two pounds flour, three-fourths lb. lard and butter, one lb. powdered white sugar, one nutmeg grated ; after the flour and butter have been incorporated, lay the sugar in and pour upon it a small tea-spoonful of saleratus dissolved ; have six eggs well beaten, and with a spoon incorporate them well together, till it can be moulded with the hands ; roll it thin, cut with a tumbler, and bake in a few minutes in a quick oven without turning.

### 76. Queen's Cake.

One pound flour, one pound sugar, one pound butter, one pound fennel, four eggs, one gill cream, with a little saleratus and nutmeg.

### 77. Dough Nuts.

One cup molasses, one cup sugar, one cup sour milk, piece of butter or lard the size of an egg, two eggs, large tea-spoonful saleratus, a little salt, flour enough to mould it stiff. Fry them in lard.

### 78. Sponge Cake.

Four large eggs, two cups flour, two of sugar—even full ; beat to a froth the whites and add them ; stir in the flour, and, without delay, put into the oven.

### 79. Rice Flour Sponge Cake.

Made like other Sponge Cake, except that you use three quarters of a pound of rice flour, thirteen eggs, leaving out four whites, and add a little salt.

### 80. Rice Griddle Cakes.

Boil one large cup of whole rice quite soft in milk, and while hot stir in a little flour, rice flour, or Indian meal ; when cold, add two or three eggs, and a little salt. Bake in small thin cakes on the griddle.

### 81. Soft Gingerbread, very nice.

Four tea-cups of flour, two cups of molasses, half a cup of butter, two cups of buttermilk, a cup of thick cream, three eggs, table spoonful of ginger, and the same of saleratus. Mix them all together with the exception of buttermilk, in which the saleratus must be dissolved and then added to the rest. It must not stand long before being sent to bake.

### 82. Mrs. Green's Gingerbread.

One pound butter, one pound sugar, one cup milk, one large table-spoonful ginger, one large tea-spoonful saleratus, flour enough to roll well.

### 83. Apple Pudding.

Line a basin with paste, tolerably thin, fill it with the apples and cover it with the paste, tie a cloth over it and boil it about an hour and a half, till the apples are done soft.

### 84. Bread Pudding.

One pound of soft bread or biscuit, soaked in one quart of milk, run through a seive or cullender; add seven eggs, three quarters of a pound of sugar, one quarter of a pound of butter, nutmeg, cinnamon, one gill of rose water, one pound raisins, half a pint of milk; bake three quarters of an hour, middling hot oven.

### 85. Rice Flour Pudding.

Take a quart of milk, add a pint of rice flour, boil them to a pap, beat up six eggs, to which add six spoonfuls of Havana sugar, and a spoonful of butter, which, when well beaten together, add them to the milk and flour; grease the pan it is to be made in, grate nutmeg over the mixture, and bake it.

### 86. Boston Pudding.

Make a good common paste. When you roll it out the last time cut off the edges till you get it of a square shape. Have ready some fruit sweetened to your taste. If cranberries, gooseberries, or dried peaches, they should be stewed. If apples, they should be stewed in a very little water, drained, and seasoned with some kind of spice to your liking. If currants, raspberries, or black-berries, they should be mashed with sugar and put into the pudding raw. Spread the fruit thick all over the sheet of paste (which must not be rolled too thin.) When it is covered all over with the fruit, roll it up and close the dough at both ends and down the last side. Tie the pudding in a cloth and boil it. Eat it hot with sugar. Some use beef suet instead of butter for making the paste.

### 87. Boiled Bread Pudding.

Grate white bread, pour boiling milk over it, and cover close. When soaked an hour or two beat it fine, and mix it with two or three eggs well beaten. Put it into a basin that will just hold it, tie a floured cloth over it, and put it in boiling water. Send it up with nice sauce.

### 88. Squash Pudding.

Run your stewed squash through a sieve, take four eggs, one pint of milk, sweeten it thoroughly, add a little rose water and cinnamon. Make a good paste, and pour the above ingredients into a deep pudding dish.

### 89. Custard Pudding.

Mix by degrees a pint of milk with a large spoonful of flour, the yolks of five eggs, and some grated lemon. Butter a basin that will exactly hold it, pour the batter in and tie a floured cloth over. Put it in boiling water over the fire, and turn it about a few minutes to prevent the eggs from going to one side. Half an hour will boil it. Serve it with sweet sauce.

### 90. Baked Rice Pudding.

Swell a coffee-cup of rice, add a quart of milk, sweeten it with brown sugar, and bake it about an hour or a little more in a quick oven or baker.

### 91. Another.

Two cups rice, two quarts milk, half cup sugar, large tea-spoonful salt; bake two hours; serve up with butter.

### 92. Fruit Rice Pudding.

Swell the rice with milk over the fire, then mix fruit of any kind with it,—currants, gooseberries, or quartered apples; put one egg in to bind the rice; boil it well and serve it with sugar.

### 93. Suet Pudding.

Chop a pound of suet, mix with it a pound and a quarter of flour, two eggs beaten separately, a little salt, and as little milk as will make it. Boil it four hours. It eats well next day cut in slices and broiled.

### 94. Plain Rice Pudding.

Wash and pick your rice, tie it in a cloth, leaving plenty of room for it to swell. Boil it an hour or more as you prefer. When done eat it with sweet sauce, or butter and sugar. Two eggs put in while it is hot, well beaten, is an improvement.

### 95. Green Corn Pudding.

Take one and a half dozen ears of green corn, split the kernels lengthwise of the ear with a sharp knife, then with a case knife scrape the corn from the cob, leaving the hulls on the cob; mix with three to four quarts of rich sweet milk; add four eggs well beat; two table-spoonfuls of sugar; salt to the taste: bake three hours. To be eaten hot, with butter.

### 96. Sago Pudding.

Boil a pint and a half of new milk, with four spoonfuls of sago, nicely washed and picked, lemon-peel, cinnamon, and nutmeg; sweeten to taste; then mix four eggs, put a paste round the dish, and bake slowly.

### 97. Another.

A large table-spoonful of sago, boiled in one quart of milk, the peel of a lemon, a little nutmeg, and four eggs. Bake it about an hour and a half.

### 98. Apple Dumpling.

Set your tin pail or kettle on the stove, put in one cup of water, cut in four large apples, one pint sour milk, one large tea-spoonful saleratus, mould your crust and spread it over the top; cover it tight; bake one hour.

### 99. Another.

Select large, fair, pleasant sour, & mellow apples, pare them, and take out the core with a small knife and fill up the place with sugar; prepare some pie crust, roll it out quite thick, and cut it into pieces just large enough to cover one apple. Lay an apple on each piece and enclose them entirely; tie them up in a thick piece of cloth that has been well floured, put them in a pot of boiling water and boil one hour ; if the boiling should stop, they will be heavy. Serve them up with sweet sauce, or butter and sugar.

### 100. Apple Pudding.

Set your tin kettle or pail on the stove, put in one cup of water, cut in four large apples ; for crust, take one pint of sour milk, one large tea-spoonful of saleratus, and flour enough to mould it up stiff, roll it out and cover it over the pudding ; boil it one hour, leaving a vent. Serve with sweet sauce.

### 101. Birds' Nest Pudding.

Put into three pints boiling milk, six crackers pounded fine, and one and a half pints of raisins ; when cool add four eggs well beaten, a little sugar, and four good sized apples, pared, with the core carefully removed. To be baked, and eaten with warm sauce.

### 102. Baked Rice Pudding.

Two cups of rice, two quarts of milk, half a cup of sugar, large tea-spoonful of salt. Bake it two hours.

### 103. Sunderland Pudding.

Eight spoonfuls of flour, six eggs, one pint of milk. Baked in cups about fifteen minutes ; sweet sauce.

### 104. Batter Pudding.

One quart of milk, three eggs, one table spoonful of salt ; beat the ingredients till free from lumps and it will not rope ; boil it one hour and a half ; if the batter be quite thin, butter the bag.

### 105. Sago Pudding.

One half cup of sago to one quart milk ; if the *white* sago bake two or three hours—if the *brown*, stew, before adding the milk ; beat four eggs, adding salt ; spice to your taste, and add more milk if quite thick with sago. Bake one hour.

### 106. Puddings in haste.

Shred suet, and put with grated bread, a few currants, the yolks of four eggs and the whites of two, some grated lemon-peel, and ginger. Mix, and make into little balls about the size and shape of an egg, with a little flour. Have ready a skillet of boiling water, and throw them in. Twenty minutes will boil them; they will rise to the top when done. Pudding sauce.

### 107. Bread and Butter Pudding.

Slice bread spread with butter, and lay it in a dish with currants between each layer; add sliced citron, orange, or lemon, if to be very nice. Pour over an unboiled custard of milk, two or three eggs, a few pimentos, and a very little preserve, two hours at least before it is to be baked; and lard it over to soak the bread. A paste round the edge makes all puddings look better, but is not necessary.

### 108. Baked Apple Pudding.

Pare and quarter four large apples; boil them tender, with the rind of a lemon, in so little water that, when done, none may remain; beat them quite fine in a mortar; add the crumb of a small roll, four ounces of butter melted, the yolks of five and whites of three eggs, juice of half a lemon, and sugar to taste; beat all together, and lay it in a dish with paste to turn out.

### 109. Plum Pudding.

Mix a pound of suet, ditto flour, half a pound of currants, ditto raisins stoned and a little cut, with spice, lemon, one egg, and milk. Will make an excellent pudding, if long boiled.

### 110. Quince Pudding.

Take six large ripe quinces; pare them, and cut out all the blemishes. Then scrape them to a pulp, and mix the pulp with half a pint of cream, and a half a pound of powdered sugar, stiring them together very hard. Beat the yolks of seven eggs, (omitting all the whites except two) and stir them gradually into the mixture, adding two wine glasses of rose water. Stir the whole well together, and bake it in a buttered dish three quarters of an hour. Grate sugar over it when cold.

### 111. Rice Milk.

Pick and wash half a pint of rice, and boil it in a quart of water till it is quite soft. Then drain it, and mix it with a quart of rich milk. You may add half a pound of whole raisins. Set it over hot coals, and stir it frequently till it boils. When it boils hard, stir in alternately two beaten eggs, and four large table-spoonfuls of brown sugar.

### 112. Plain Rice Pudding.

Boil three cups of rice in two quarts of milk till soft, then add two quarts of cold milk, eight eggs beat light, a quarter pound of butter, two nutmegs, and sugar to the taste.

### 113. Another.

Boil in water one pound ground rice till soft, add four quarts of milk, sixteen eggs, twelve ounces butter, two pounds raisins ; bake two hours.

### 114. Bread Pudding.

Cut one loaf of bread in fine pieces, sprinkle with a little salt, boil two quarts of milk and pour over, cover close until well soaked, mash it well, add six eggs, one pound butter; some cinnamon or nutmeg, sweeten it, bake it in a quick oven one hour and a half.

### 115. Flour Pudding.

Beat one dozen eggs light, add two quarts of milk, a little salt, mix with wheat flour to a batter, beat it well, pour into a bag and boil four hours ; two pounds of currants added to it is a great improvement, but it is very good without.

### 116. Plum Pudding boiled.

Three quarts of flour, a little salt, twelve eggs, two pounds of raisins, one pound of beef suet chopped fine, one quart of milk ; put into a strong cloth floured ; boil three hours. Eat with sauce.

### 117. Apple Pudding.

Pare and stew three pints of apples, mash them, add eight eggs, half a pound of butter, sugar and nutmeg or grated lemon peel ; bake on short crust.

### 118. Boiled Apple Pudding.

Pare, core, and quarter as many fine juicy apples as will weigh two pounds when done. Strew among them a quarter of a pound of brown sugar, add a grated nut-meg, and the juice and yellow peel of a large lemon. Prepare a paste of suet and flour, in the proportion of a pound of chopped suet to two pounds of flour. Roll it out of moderate thickness; lay the apples in the cen-tre, and close the paste nicely over them in the form of a large dumpling; tie it in a cloth and boil it three hours. Send it to the table hot, and eat it with cream sauce, or with butter and sugar.

### 119. Indian Pudding.

Three quarts of scalded milk, fourteen spoonfuls fine Indian meal, stir well; when cool add eight eggs, one pound butter, spice and sugar; bake four hours.

### 120. Another, and a cheap one.

Scald four cups of Indian meal with boiling water, add two cups molasses and milk, (each,) half pound raisins, a little suet chopped fine, four eggs, and some ground cinnamon.

### 121. Suet Pudding.

Mince very fine as much beef suet as will make two large table-spoonfuls. Grate two handfuls of bread-crumbs; boil a quart of milk and pour it hot on the bread. Cover it, and set it aside to steep for half an hour; then put it to cool. Beat eight eggs very light; stir the suet, and three table-spoonfuls of flour alternately into the bread and milk, and add by degrees, the eggs. Lastly stir in a table-spoonful of powdered nutmeg and cinnamon mixed. Pour it into a bag that has been dipped in hot water and floured; tie it firmly; put it into a pot of boiling water and boil it two hours. Do not take it up till immediately before it is wanted, and send it to the table hot. Eat it with sauce or with molasses.

### 122. Plain Suet Dumplings.

Sift two pounds of flour into a pan, and add a salt-spoon of salt. Mince very fine one pound of beef suet, and rub it into a stiff dough with a little cold water. Then roll it out an inch thick or rather more. Cut it into dumplings with the edge of a tumbler. Put them into a pot of boiling water, and let them boil an hour and a half. Send them to the table hot, to eat with boiled loin of mutton, or with molasses after the meat is removed.

### 123. Boiled Milk Pudding.

Pour a pint of new milk, boiling hot, on three spoonfuls of fine flour, beat the flour and milk for half an hour, then put in three eggs and beat it a little longer, grate in half a tea-spoonful of ginger, dip the cloth in boiling water, butter it well, and flour it, put it in the pudding, tie it close up, and boil it an hour. It requires great care when you turn it out. Pour over it thick melted butter.

### 124. Plain Pudding.

Boil half a pint of milk with a bit of cinnamon, four eggs with the whites well beaten, the rind of a lemon grated, half a pound of suet chopped fine, as much bread as will do; pour your milk on the bread and suet, keep mixing it till cold, then put in the lemon peel, eggs, a little sugar, and some nutmeg grated fine. It may be either baked or boiled.

### 125. Ground Rice Pudding.

Boil four ounces of ground rice in water, till it be soft, then beat the yolks of four eggs and put to them a pint of cream, four ounces of sugar, and a quarter of a pound of butter; mix them all well together; you may either boil or bake it.

### 126. Little Citron Puddings.

Take half a pint of cream, one spoonful of fine flour, two ounces of sugar, a little nutmeg, mix them all well together, with the yolks of three eggs, put it in tea-cups, and stick in it two ounces of citron cut very thin; bake them in a pretty quick oven.

### 127. A Baked Bread Pudding.

Take a stale five cent loaf of bread; cut off all the crust, and grate or rub the crumbs as fine as possible. Boil a quart of rich milk, and pour it hot over the bread; then stir in a quarter of a pound of butter, and the same quantity of sugar, with a glass of rose-water. Or you may omit the latter and substitute the grated peel of a large lemon. Add a table-spoonful of mixed cinnamon and nutmeg powdered. Stir the whole very well, cover it, and set it away for half an hour. Then let it cool. Beat seven or eight eggs very light, and stir them gradually into the mixture after it is cold. Then butter a deep dish, and bake the pudding an hour.

### 128. Wheat Meal Pudding.

One quart of boiling water, one large tea-spoonful of salt, made stiff with wheat meal: served up with cream or sweet sauce.

### 129. Bird's Nest Sago Pudding.

Soak half a pint of sago in three pints of water, stirring it occasionally until it is uniformly swelled. Pare and core ten or twelve apples, fill the holes in the centre and put them, without piling them one over another, in a pudding dish, so that the sago will just cover them. The sago may then be poured on and the pudding baked until the apples are soft.

### 130. Rice Flour Pudding.

Boil one pint of milk, mix two table-spoonfuls of rice flour with a little cold milk, stir it in while the milk is boiling, afterwards add a small piece of butter, five eggs, one nutmeg, one glass of preserve juice, the juice and peel of one lemon, and sugar to your taste.

### 131. Whortleberry Pudding in Winter.

Put the berries in a bottle, then cork and seal it, place the bottle in a kettle of cold water, and gradually let it boil. As soon as it boils, take it off and let it cool; then take the bottles out, and put them away for winter use.

Gooseberries, Plums, and Currants, may be preserved in the same manner.

### 132. Observations on Making Puddings.

The outside of a boiled pudding often tastes disagreeably; which arises by the cloth not being nicely washed and kept in a dry place. It should be dipped in boiling water, squeezed dry, and floured when to be used. If bread, it should be tied loose; if batter, tight over. The water should boil quick when the pudding is put in; and it should be moved about for a minute, lest the ingredients should not mix. Batter pudding should be strained through a coarse sieve, when all is mixed; in others, the eggs separately. The pans and basins must be always buttered. A pan of cold water should be ready, and the pudding dipped in as soon as it comes out of the pot, and then it will not adhere to the cloth.

### 133. Pudding Sauce.

One pint sugar, table-spoonful of vinegar, piece of butter size of an egg, boil fifteen minutes, add one table-spoonful of rose-water, little nutmeg, boil with the sugar in nearly a pint of water, a large table-spoonful of flour.

### 134. Cold Sauce.

Take equal quantities of powdered sugar and butter: knead them together, make the mixture in a lump, and grate a nutmeg on it.

### 135. Common Paste for Pies.

A pound and a half of sifted flour, three quarters of a pound of butter washed; this will make a crust for one large pie or two small ones. Sift the flour into a pan, cut the butter into two equal parts, cut one half into the flour in very small pieces, mix it well with the flour, wetting it gradually with a little cold water. Spread some flour on your moulding board, take the lump of paste out of the pan, flour your rolling-pin, and roll out the paste into a large sheet. Then stick it over with the remaining half of the butter in small pieces and laid at equal distances; throw on a little flour, fold up the sheets of paste, flour it slightly, and roll it out again. Then fold it up and cut it half or four according to the size of your pie-plates, pressing rather harder on your rolling-pin. Some think it makes common paste more light and crisp to beat it hard on both sides with the rolling-pin after you give it the first rolling when all the butter is in.

### 136. Veal Pie.

Cut your veal up in small pieces, boil it an hour, season it with salt and pepper and a small piece of butter; mix your flour with sour milk, saleratus, and a small piece of lard, and mould it for the crust, line the sides of a tin dish or basin with the crust, put the meat in, and fill up the basin with the gravy as full as you can handle it, shake some flour in it, and cover it over with the crust, leaving a hole in the centre, for a vent. Bake from one and a half to two hours. If preferred, cream tarter crust may be used : see cream tarter bread.

### 137. Common Mince Pie.

Boil a piece of lean fresh beef very tender, when cold chop it very fine ; then take three times the quantity of apples, pared and cored and chopped fine ; mix the meat with it, and add raisins, allspice, salt, sugar, cinnamon, and molasses, to suit the taste ; incorporate the articles well together, and it will improve by standing over night, if the weather is cool ; a very little ginger improves the flavor. Small pieces of butter, sliced over the mince before laying on the top crust, will make them keep longer.

### 138. Wisconsin Mince Pies.

Take the usual quantity of meat, and substitute *beets* for apples, put in only one third the quantity of the latter, — boil the beets, pickle them in vinegar twelve hours, chop them very fine, and add the vinegar they were pickled in. Add one-eighth of grated bread, and spice to suit you.

### 139. Pumpkin Pie.

Take out the seeds and pare the pumpkin ; stew, and strain it through a coarse seive. Take two quarts of scalded milk and eight eggs, and stir your pumpkin into it ; sweeten it with sugar or molasses. Salt it, and season with ginger, cinnamon, or grated lemon peel to your taste. Bake with a bottom crust. Crackers, pounded fine, are a good substitute for eggs.

### 140. Dried Pumpkin.

Boil and sift the pumpkin, spread it out thin on tin plates and dry hard in a warm oven. It will keep good the year round ; when wanted for use it may be soaked in milk.

### 141. Carrot Pie.

A very good pie may be made of carrots in the same way that you make pumpkin pies.

4

### 142. Apple Pie.

Peel the apples, slice them thin, pour a little molasses, and sprinkle some sugar over them, grate on some lemon-peel, or nutmeg. If you wish to make them richer, put a little butter on the top.

### 143. Green Apple Pie.

Peel and stew the apples, mash them fine with sugar, a little butter, and grated nutmeg, or lemon peel; bake in rich crust and quick oven, but not hot enough to scorch.

### 144. Rhubarb Pie.

Pull the rhubarb from the root instead of cutting it, peel off the skin from the stalk and cut it into small pieces, put them in the pie with plenty of brown sugar, you can hardly put in too much. Cover the pie, and bake like apple, in a deep plate.

### 145. Mutton Pie.

Cut steaks from a loin of mutton, beat them and remove some of the fat, season it well, and put a little water at the bottom of the dish. Cover the whole with a pretty thick paste, and bake it.

### 146. Chicken Pie.

Cut up your chicken, parboil it, season it in the pot, take up the meat, put in a flour thickening, and scald the gravy, make the crust of sour milk made sweet with saleratus, put in a piece of butter or lard the size of an egg; cream is preferable to sour milk, if you have it. Take a large tin pan, line it with the crust, put in your meat, and pour in the gravy from the pot, make it nearly full, cover it over with crust and leave a vent; bake it in a moderate oven two hours, or two and a half.

### 147. Rice Pie.

Boil your rice soft, put one egg to each pie, one table spoonful of sugar, a little salt and nutmeg.

### 148. Custard Pie.

For a large pie put in three eggs, heaping table spoonful of sugar, one pint and a half of milk, a little salt, and some nutmeg grated on. For crust use common pastry.

### 149. Custard without Eggs.

One quart new milk, four table spoonfuls flour, two do. sugar, season with nutmeg or cinnamon, and add a little salt. Set the milk over the fire, and when it boils pour in the flour, which should be previously stirred up in a little cold milk. When it is thoroughly scalded, add the sugar, spice, and salt, and bake it either in crust or cups.

### 150. Rice Custard.

Put into a pan over the fire three pints of new milk, mix in a little cold milk, a tea-cupful of ground rice, and when the milk boils, pour in the rice and let it scald thoroughly, then add half a cupful of sugar and a little salt, season with cinnamon, and bake as above.

### 151. Baked Custard.

Two quarts of milk, twelve eggs, twelve ounces sugar, four spoonfuls of rose-water, one nutmeg.

### 152. Cream Custard.

Eight eggs beat and put into two quarts of cream, sweetened to the taste, a nutmeg, and a little cinnamon.

### 153. Cranberry Tarts.

Stew your cranberries, when done add same quantity of sugar, make a rich pastry, roll it thin, make small tarts.

### 154. Whortleberry Pie.

Make common paste, line a deep plate with it, put in your berries, cover them over thick with sugar, a little butter sliced on adds to the flavor, cover it over with the crust, and bake it an hour. Very good pies may be made in the same way of Cherries, Blackberries, or Raspberries.

### 155. Lemon Pie.

Take one lemon and a half, cut them up fine, one cup of molasses, half a cup of sugar, two eggs, mix them together, prepare your plate, with a crust in the bottom, put in half the materials, lay over a crust, then put in the rest of the materials, and cover the whole with another crust.

### 156. Roasting Meats.

The first preparation for roasting is to take care that the spit be properly cleaned with sand and water ; nothing else. When it has been well scoured with this, dry it with a clean cloth. If spits are wiped clean as soon as the meat is drawn from them, and while they are hot, a very little cleaning will be required.

Make up the fire in time ; let it be proportioned to the dinner to be dressed, and about three or four inches longer at each end than the thing to be roasted, or the ends of the meat cannot be done nice and brown.

A cook must be as particular to proportion her fire to the business she has to do as a chemist : the degree of heat most desirable for dressing the different sorts of food ought to be attended to with the utmost precision.

Never put meat down to a burned up fire if you can possibly avoid it ; but should the fire become fierce, place the spit at a considerable distance and allow a little more time.

Preserve the fat by covering it with paper for this purpose, called " kitchen paper," and tie it on with a fine twine ; pins and skewers can by no means be allowed, they are so many taps to let out the gravy ; besides, the paper often starts from them and catches fire, to the great injury of the meat.

If the thing to be roasted be thin and tender, the fire should be little and brisk ; when you have a large joint to roast, make up a sound, strong fire, equally good in every part, or your meat cannot be equally roasted, nor have that uniform color which constitutes the beauty of good roasting.

Half an hour before your meat is done, make some gravy, and just before you take it up put it nearer the fire to brown it. If you wish to froth it, paste it, and dredge it with flour carefully ; you cannot do this delicacy nice without a very good light. The common fault seems to be using too much flour. The meat should have a fine light varnish of froth, not the appearance of being covered with a paste. Those who are particular about the froth use butter instead of drippings.

### 157. Baking Meats.

Baking is one of the cheapest and most convenient ways of dressing a dinner in small families ; and I may say, that the oven is often the only kitchen a poor man has, if he wishes to enjoy a joint of meat.

I do not mean to deny the superior excellence of roasting to baking; but some joints when baked, so nearly approach to the same when roasted, that I have known them to be carried to the table, and eaten as such with great satisfaction.

Legs and loins of pork, legs of mutton, fillets of veal, and many other joints, will bake to great advantage, if the meat be good; I mean well-fed, rather inclined to be fat; if the meat be poor, no baker can give satisfaction.

When baking a poor joint of meat, before it has been half baked, I have seen it start from the bone and shrivel up as scarcely to be believed.

Besides those joints above mentioned, I shall enumerate a few baked dishes which I can particularly recommend.

A pig, when prepared for baking, should have its ears and tail covered with buttered paper properly fastened on, and a bit of butter tied up in a piece of linen to baste the back with, otherwise it will be apt to blister ; with a proper share of attention from the cook, I consider this way equal to a roasted one.

A goose prepared the same as for roasting, taking care to have it on a stand, and when half done to turn the other side upwards. A duck the same.

A ham (if not too old) put in soak for an hour, taken out and wiped, crust made sufficient to cover it all over, and baked in a moderately heated oven, cuts fuller of gravy, and of a finer flavor, than a boiled one. I have been in the habit of baking small codfish, haddock, and mackerel, with a dust of flour, and some bits of butter put on them ; eels, when large and stuffed ; herrings and sprats, in a brown pan, with vinegar and a little spice, and tied over with paper. A rabbit, prepared the same way as for roasting, with a few pieces of butter, and a little drop of milk put into the dish, and basted several times, will be found nearly equal to roasting ; or cut it up, season it properly, put it into a jar or pan, and cover it over and bake it in a moderate oven for about three hours.

The time each of the above articles should take, depends much upon the state of the oven, of which the cook must be the judge. The preparation of the articles, and the heating of the oven, should both be carried along together.

### 158. Broiling Meats.

Cleanliness is extremely essential in the mode of cookery.

Keep your gridiron quite clean between the bars, and bright on the top: when it is hot, wipe it well with a linen cloth just before you use it, rub the bars with clean mutton suet, to prevent the meat being marked by the gridiron.

Take care to prepare your fire in time, so that it may burn quite clear: a brisk and clear fire is indispensible, or you cannot give your meat that browning which constitutes the perfection of this mode of cookery, and gives a relish to food it cannot receive in any other way.

The chops or slices should be from half to three-quarters of an inch in thickness; if thicker they will be done too much on the outside before the inside is done enough.

Be diligently attentive to watch the moment that any thing is done: never hasten any thing that is broiling, lest you make smoke and spoil it.

Let the bars of the gridiron be all hot through, but yet not burning hot upon the surface; this is the perfect and fine condition of the gridiron.

Upright gridirons are the best, as they can be used at any fire without fear of smoke; and the gravy is preserved in the trough under them.

N. B. Broils must be brought to table hot as possible; set a dish to heat when you put the chops on the gridirons, from whence to the mouth their progress must be as quick as possible.

### 159. Boiling Meats.

This most simple of culinary processes is not often performed in perfection. It does not require quite so much nicety and attention as roasting; to skim the pot well, and keep it really boiling (the slower the better) all the while, to know how long is required for doing the joint, &c., and to take it up at the critical moment when it is done enough, comprehends almost the whole art and mystery. This however demands a patient and perpetual vigilance, of which few persons are capable.

The cook must take especial care that the water really boils all the while she is cooking, or she will be deceived in the time; and make up a sufficient fire at first to last all the time, without much mending or stirring. A frugal cook will manage with much less fire for boiling than she uses for roasting.

When the pot is coming to the boil there will always, from the cleanest meat and the cleanest water, rise a *scum* to the top of it, proceeding partly from the water; this must be carefully taken off as soon as it rises.

On this depends the good appearance of all boiled things. When you have skimmed well, put in some cold water, which will throw up the rest of the scum.

The oftener it is skimmed, and the cleaner the top of the water is kept, the sweeter and the cleaner will be the meat.

If left alone, it soon boils down and sticks to the meat, which instead of looking delicately white and nice, will have that coarse and filthy appearance we have too often to complain of, and the butcher and poulterer be blamed for the carelessness of the cook in not skimming her pot.

Many put in *milk*, to make what they boil look white: but this does more harm than good: others wrap it up in a cloth; but these are needless precautions; if the scum be attentively removed, meat will have much more delicate color and finer flavor than it has when muffled up. This may give rather more trouble, but those who wish to excel in their art must only consider how the processes of it can be most perfectly performed; a cook who has a proper pride and pleasure in her business, will make this her maxim on all occasions.

It is desirable that meat for boiling be of an equal thickness, or, before thicker parts are done enough the thiner will be done too much.

Put your meat into *cold* water, in proportion of about a quart of water to a pound of meat; it should be covered with water during the whole process of boiling but not drowned in it; the less water, provided the meat be covered with it, the more savory will be the meat, and the better will be the broth.

The water should be heated gradually, according to

the thickness, &c., of the article boiled. For instance, a leg of mutton of ten pounds weight, should be placed over a moderate fire, which will gradually make the water hot, without causing it to boil for about forty minutes; if the water boils much sooner, the meat will be hardened, and shrink up, as if it was scorched; by keeping the water a certain time heating without boiling, the fibres of the meat are dilated, and it yields a quantity of scum, which must be taken off as soon as it rises.

The old rule of fifteen minutes to a pound of meat, we think rather too little; the slower it boils, the tenderer, the plumper, and whiter it will be.

For those who choose their food thoroughly cooked, (which all will who have any regard for their stomachs,) twenty minutes to a pound for fresh, and rather more for salted meat, will not be found too much for gentle simmering by the side of the fire, allowing more or less time according to the thickness of the joint, and the coldness of the weather; to know the state of which, let a thermometer be placed in the pantry; and when it falls below forty degrees, tell your cook to give rather more time in both roasting and boiling, always remembering, the slower it boils the better.

Without some practice it is difficult to teach any art: and cooks seem to suppose they must be right, if they put meat into a pot, and set it over the fire for a certain time, making no allowance whether it simmers without a bubble or boils a gallop.

Fresh killed meat will take much longer time boiling than that which has been kept till it is what the butchers call *ripe;* and longer in *cold* than in *warm* weather; if it be *frozen* it must be thawed before boiling as before roasting; if it be fresh-killed, it will be tough and hard, if you stew it ever so gently. In cold weather, the night before the day you dress it, bring it into a place of which the temperature is not less than forty-five degrees of Fahrenheit's thremometer.

The size of the boiling-pots should be adapted to what they are to contain; the larger the sauce-pan, the more room it takes upon the fire, and a larger quantity of water requires a proportionate increase of fire to boil it.

In small families we recommend block-tin sauce-pans, &c., as lightest and safest. If proper care be taken of them, and they are well cleaned, they are by far the cheapest; the purchase of a new tin sauce-pan being little more than the expense of tinning a copper one.

Let the covers of your boiling-pots fit close, not only to prevent unnecessary evaporation of the water, but to prevent the escape of the nutritive matter, which must then remain either in the meat or in the broth; and the smoke is prevented from insinuating itself under the edge of the lid, and so giving the meat a bad taste.

### 160.  Frying Meats.

Frying is often a convenient mode of cookery; it may be performed by a fire which will not do for roasting or boiling; and by the introduction of a pan between the meat and the fire things get more equally dressed. A frying-pan should be about four inches deep, with a perfectly flat and thick bottom, twelve inches long and nine broad, with perpendicular sides, and must be half filled with fat; good frying is, in fact, boiling in fat. To make sure that the pan is quite clean, rub a little fat over it, and then make it warm, and wipe it out with a clean cloth.

Be very particular in frying, never to use any oil, butter, lard, or drippings, but what is quite clean, fresh, and free from salt. Any thing dirty spoils the looks: any thing bad-tasted or stale, spoils the flavor; and salt prevents its browning.

For general purposes, and especially for fish, clean fresh lard is not near so expensive as oil or clarified butter, and does almost as well. Butter often burns before you are aware of it; and what you fry will get a dark and dirty appearance.

To know when the fat is of a proper heat, according to what you are to fry, is the real secret in frying.

To fry fish, parsley, potatoes, or any thing that is watery, your fire must be very clear, and the fat quite hot; which you may be pretty sure of, when it has done hissing, and is still.  We cannot insist too strongly on this point; if the fat is not very hot, you cannot fry fish either to a good color, or firm and crisp.

### 161.  Soups.

To extract the strength from the meat, long and slow boiling is necessary, but care must be taken that the pot is never off the boil. All soups are better for being made the day before they are to be used, and they should then be strained into earthen pans. When soup has jellied in the pan, it should not be removed into another, as breaking it will occasion its becoming sour sooner than it would otherwise do: when in danger of not keeping, it should be boiled up.

### 162. To Roast Pork.

When you roast a loin, take a sharp penknife and cut the skin across, to make the crackling eat the better.— Roast a leg of pork thus : take a knife and score it; stuff the knuckle part with sage and onion, chopped fine with pepper and salt; or cut a hole under the twist, and put the sage, &c., there, and skewer it up. Roast it crisp. Make apple sauce, and send up in a boat; then have a little drawn gravy to put in the dish. This is called a mock goose. The spring, or hand of pork, if young, roasted like a pig, eats very well, otherwise it is better boiled. The spare-rib should be basted with a bit of butter, a little flour, and some sage : never make any sauce to it but apple. To every pound allow a quarter of an hour : for example, a joint of twelve pounds weight will require three hours, and so on. If it be a thin piece of that weight, two honrs will roast it.

### 163. To Roast Veal.

Be careful to roast veal of a fine brown color; if a large joint, have a good fire; if small, a little brisk fire. If a fillet or loin, be sure to paper the fat, that you lose as little of that as possible : lay it at some distance from the fire, till it is soaked, then lay it near the fire. When you lay it down, paste it well with good butter; and when it is near done, paste it again, and drudge it with a little flour. The breast must be roasted with the caul on till it is done enough; skewer the sweet bread on the back side of the breast. When it is nigh done, take off the caul, paste it, and dredge it with a little flour. Veal takes much about the same time in roasting as pork.

### 194. To Roast Beef.

Paper the top, and baste it well, while roasting, with its own dripping, and throw a handful of salt on it.

When you see the smoke draw to the fire, it is near enough ; take off the paper, baste it well, and drudge it with a little flour to make a fine froth. Never salt roast meat before you lay it to the fire, for it draws out the gravy. If you would keep it a few days before you dress it, dry it with a cloth, and hang it where the air will come to it. When you take up the meat, garnish the dish with horse-radish.

### 165. To Roast a Pig.

Spit a pig, and lay it to the fire, which must be a very good one at each end, or hang a flat iron in the middle of the grate. Before you lay the pig down, take a little sage shred small, a piece of butter as big as a walnut, and pepper and salt, put them in the pig, and sew it up with a coarse thread; flour it well over, and keep flouring till the eyes drop out, or you find the crackling hard. Be sure to save all the gravy that comes out of it, by setting basins or pans under the pig in the dripping pan, as soon as the gravy begins to run. When the pig is done enough, stir the fire up ; take a coarse cloth with about a quarter of a pound of butter in it, and rub the pig over till the crackling is crisp, then take it up. Lay it in a dish, and with a sharp knife cut off the head, then cut the pig in two, before you draw out the spit. Cut the ears off the head, and lay them at each end ; cut the under jaw in two, and lay the parts on each side : melt some good butter, take the gravy you saved and put in it, boil it, pour it in the dish with the brains bruised fine, and the sage mixed together, and then send it to the table. If just killed, a pig will require an hour to roast ; If killed the day before, an hour and a quarter. If a very large one, an hour and a half. But the best way to judge is when the eyes drop out, and the skin is grown very hard ; then rub it with a coarse cloth, with a good piece of butter rolled in it, till the crackling is crisp, and of a light brown color.

### 166. To Roast Mutton and Lamb.

In roasting mutton, the loin, haunch, and saddle, must be done as beef; but all other parts of mutton and lamb must be roasted with a quick clear fire ; paste it when you lay it down ; and just before you take it up,

dredge it with a little flour ; but be sure not to use too
much, for that takes away all the fine taste of the meat.
Some choose to skin a loin of mutton, and roast it brown.
Be sure always to take the skin off a breast of mutton.
A leg of mutton of six pounds will take an hour at a
quick fire ; if frosty weather, an hour and a quarter :
nine pounds, an hour and a half; a leg of twelve pounds
will take two hours ; if frosty, two hours and a half.

### 167.  To Roast Venison.

Spit a haunch of venison, and butter well four sheets
of paper, two of which put on the haunch ; then make
a paste with flour, butter, and water, roll it out half as
big as the haunch, and put it over the fat part; then put
the other two sheets of paper on, and tie them with pack
thread ; lay it to a brisk fire, and paste it well all the
time of roasting.  If a large haunch of twenty-four
pounds, it will take three hours and a half, unless there
is a very large fire ; then three hours will do : smaller
in proportion.

### 168.  To Roast a Tongue or Udder.

Parboil it first, then roast it, stick eight or ten cloves
about it, paste it with butter, and have gravy and sweet
sauce.  An udder eats very deliciously done the same
way.

### 169.  Spare Rib.

Should be basted with a very little butter and a little
flour and then sprinkled with a little dried sage crum-
bled.  Apple-sauce and potatoes for roasted pork.

### 170.  Beef A-La-Mode.

Choose a piece of thick flank of a fine heifer or ox,
cut into long slices some fat bacon, but quite free from
yellow ; let each bit be near an inch thick ; dip them
into vinegar, and then into a seasoning ready prepared,
of salt, black pepper, alspice, and a clove, all in a fine
powder, with parsley, chives, thyme, savory, and knotted
marjorum, shred as small as possible, and well mixed.
With a sharp knife make holes deep enough to let in the
larding, then rub the beef over with the seasoning, and
bind it up tight with tape.  Set it in a well tinned pot
over a fire or rather stove ; three or four onions must be

fried brown and put to the beef, with two or three carrots, one turnip, a head or two of celery, and a small quantity of water, let it simmer gently ten or twelve hours, or till extremely tender, turning the meat twice.

### 171. Leg of Veal.

Let the fillet be cut large or small, as best suits the number of your company. Take out the bone, fill the space with fine stuffing, and let it be skewered quite round ; and send the large side uppermost. When half roasted, if not before, put a paper over the fat ; and take care to allow a sufficient time, and put it a good distance from the fire, as the meat is very solid ; serve with melted butter poured over it.

### 172. To Boil a Ham.

Put a ham in the copper whilst the water is cold ; be careful that it boils slowly. A ham of twenty pounds takes four hours and a half, larger and smaller in proportion. Keep the copper well skimmed. A green ham wants no soaking ; but an old one must be soaked sixteen hours, in a large tub of soft water.

### 173. An excellent way of doing Tongues to eat cold.

Season with common salt and saltpetre, brown sugar, pepper, cloves, mace, and alspice, in fine powder for a fortnight ; then take away the pickle, put the tongue in a small pan, lay some butter on it ; cover it with brown crust, and bake slowly till so tender that a straw would go through it.

### 174. To Bake a Pig.

Lay it in a dish, flour it all over well, and rub it over with butter, butter the dish you lay it in, and put it in the oven. When it is done, draw it out to the oven's mouth and rub it over with a buttery cloth ; then put it in the oven again till it is dry. Now take it out and lay it in a dish, cut it up, take a little veal gravy ; and having taken off the fat in the dish it was baked in, there will be some good gravy at the bottom ; put that to it with a little piece of butter rolled in flour ; boil it up, and put it in the dish with the brains and sage in the belly. Some like a pig brought whole to the table, then you are only to put what sauce you like in the dish.

### 175. To keep Meat hot.

If the meat is done before the company is ready, set the dish over a pan of boiling water; cover a dish with a deep cover so as not to touch the meat, and throw a cloth over all. Thus you may keep meat hot along time and it is better than over roasting and spoiling it. The steam of the water keeps it hot and does not draw the gravy out: whereas, if you set the dish of meat any time over coals it will dry up all the gravy and spoil the meat.

### 176. To Boil a Leg of Pork.

Salt it eight or ten days: when it is to be dressed weigh it; let it lie half an hour in cold water to make it white; allow a quarter of an hour for every pound, and half an hour over from the time it boils up; skim it as soon as it boils, and frequently after. Allow water enough. Save some of it to make peas-soup. Some boil it in a very nice cloth, floured; which gives a very delicate look. It should be small and of a fine grain.— Serve peas-pudding and turnips with it.

### 177. Round of Beef.

Should be carefully salted, and wet with the pickle for eight or ten days. The bone should be cut out first, and the beef skewered and tied up to make it quite round. It may be stuffed with parsley, if approved; in which case the holes to admit the parsley must be made with a sharp pointed knife, and the parsley coarsely cut and stuffed in tight. As soon as it boils it should be skimmed, and afterwards kept boiling very gently.

### 178. To Boil a Tongue.

Put a tongue, if soft, in a pot over night, and do not let it boil till about three hours before dinner, then boil till dinner time; if fresh out of the pickle, two hours and a half, and put it in when the water boils.

### 179. To Boil Calf's Head.

Clean it very nicely, and soak it in water, till it looks very white; take out the tongue to salt, and the brains to make a little dish. Boil the head extremely tender; then strew it over with crumbs and chopped parsley, and brown them; or if liked better, leave one side plain.—

Bacon and greens are to be served to eat with it. The brains must be boiled; and then mixed with melted butter, scalded sage chopped, pepper, and salt. If any of the head is left, it may be hashed next day, and a few slices of bacon just warmed and put round.

### 180. Stuffing---No. 1.

Quarter of a pound of clear fat pork chopped fine, eight or ten crackers pounded fine, two eggs, one cup of flour, one pint of milk or water, sage, pepper, and salt to your taste.

### 181. Stuffing---No. 2.

Take dry pieces of bread or crackers, chop them fine, put in a small piece of butter, or a little cream, with sage, pepper, and salt, one egg, and a small quantity of flour, moistened with milk.

### 182. Roast Turkey.

Let the turkey be picked clean, and washed and wiped dry, inside and out. Have your stuffing, No. 2, prepared, and fill the crop and then the body full, sew it up, and put it on a spit, and roast it before a moderate fire, three hours.

Serve up with cranberry or apple sauce, turnip sauce, squash, and a small Indian pudding, or dumplings boiled hard, is a good substitue for bread.

### 183. Boiled Dish---Meat.

Corned beef should be boiled three hours, pork two hours. Beets need as much boiling as the beef in the winter, one hour will do in the summer when they are more tender; carrots, cabbage and turnips, each an hour, parsnips forty-five minutes, potatoes twenty to thirty minutes.

### 184. To Roast Geese and Ducks.

Take sage, wash and pick it, and an onion; chop them fine, with pepper and salt, and put them in the belly; let the goose be clean picked, and wiped dry with a cloth, inside and out; put it down to the fire, and roast it brown. Serve it in a dish with brown gravy, apple-sauce in a boat, and some gravy in another. Ducks are dressed in the same way.

### 185. Meat Soup.

Scraps and crumbs of meat make a very good dinner, when made into a soup. Put all your crumbs of meat into the dinner pot. Slice in two onions, a carrot, put in a little salt and pepper, and water enough to cover it; then cover it over with a crust, made with cream tartar. See No. 9.

### 186. To Boil a Turkey.

Prepare and stuff the turkey, the same as for roasting, boil it two hours, with a piece of striped pork, a nice head of cabbage, flat turnips, and potatoes. Serve up with butter gravy.

### 187. To Broil Beaf Steak.

Cut slices of beef as thick as your hand, put it on the gridiron, and set it over a bed of live coals free from any smoke, and broil ten minutes; when done, take it up on a platter, or deep plate, and put pieces of butter over the meat; it should be broiled the last thing before the family sit down, and brought to the table hot.

### 188. To Broil Pork.

Cut your pork in slices, pour on some boiling water, let it drain, roll it in some flour, and broil it brown.

### 189. To Boil a Shoulder of Mutton with Oysters.

Hang it some days, then salt it well for two days, bone it and sprinkle it with pepper and a bit of mace pounded; lay some oysters over it, and roll the meat up tight and tie it. Stew it in a small quantity of water, with an onion and a few pepper corns, till quite tender. Have ready a little good gravy, and some oysters stewed in it, thicken this with flour and butter, and pour over the mutton when the tape is taken off. The stew-pan should be kept close covered.

### 190. Gravy Sauce.

Beef of good quality, and roasted with care, affords the best sauce for the meat. Free it of the sediment and fat, add a little salt, and a little flour, and boil it. A little butter may be added to the veal gravy.

### 191. To Corn Beef or Pork.

Wash the beef well, after it has lain awhile in cold water. Then drain and examine it, take out all the kernels, and rub it plentifully with salt. It will imbibe the salt more readily after being washed. In cold weather warm the salt by placing it before the fire. This will cause it to penetrate the meat more thoroughly. In summer do not attempt to corn any beef that has not been fresh killed, and even then it will not keep more than a day and a half or two days. Wash and dry it, and rub a great deal of salt well into it. Cover it carefully, and keep it in a cold dry cellar.

### 192. Chicken Pot Pie.

Wash and cut the chicken into joints; take out the breast bone; boil them about twenty minutes; take them up, wash out your kettle; fry two or three slices of fat salt pork, and put in the bottom of the kettle; then put in the chicken, with about three pints of water, a piece of butter the size of an egg; sprinkle in a little pepper, and cover over the top with a light crust. It will require one hour to cook.

### 193. Cooking Potatoes.

Select the potatoes you design for dinner the day previous; pare them and throw them into cold water and let them stand three or four hours; then, at a proper time before dinner, put them into boiling water; and when they have sufficiently boiled, turn off all the water, leave off the cover and hang them over the fire to dry. When the steam has passed off they will then be in the best possible condition for eating. By this mode, potatoes even of a watery and inferior quality, become mealy and good.

### 194. Another Way.

Put them in a pot or kettle without a lid, with water just sufficient to cover them. After the water has come nearly to boil, pour it off, and replace it with cold water, into which throw a good portion of salt. The cold water sends the heat from the surface to the heart and makes the potatoes meally. After they are boiled and the water is poured off, let them stand on the fire ten or fifteen minutes to dry.

4*

### 195. Bread Sauce.

Take four ounces of grated stale bread; pour over it sufficient milk to cover it, and let it soak about three quarters of an hour, or till it becomes incorporated with the milk. Then add a dozen corns of black pepper, a little salt, and a piece of butter the size of a walnut. Pour on a little more milk, and give it a boil. Serve it up in a sauce-boat, and eat it with roast wild fowl, or roast pig. Instead of the pepper you may boil in it a handful of dried currants, well picked, washed, and floured.

### 196. Green Peas.

Should be young and fresh shelled; wash them clean; put them into a bag, and that into a plenty of boiling water, with a little salt, and a tea-spoonful of pounded loaf sugar, boil them till tender. It takes from half an hour to one hour to boil them. Never let them stand in the water after they are done. Season them with a little butter and salt.

### 197. To Boil Fish.

To boil fresh fish, lay it on a strainer, or sew up the fish in a cloth, to prevent its breaking to pieces when you take it up. Put it into cold water, skin side down, to six pounds fish put in three or four spoonfuls of salt, and a little vinegar may be put in the water to make the fish more firm; boil from fifteen to thirty minutes. Serve up with butter gravy.

### 198. To Broil Fish.

Rub the bars of the gridiron over with a little butter, lay your fish on skin side down, and do not turn till nearly done through. Fish should broil slowly; put pieces of butter on, after it is taken up on the platter, and avoid laying one piece over another.

### 199. To Fry Fish.

The fat from salt pork is best; have enough to cover the fish, and it should be hot when the fish is laid in; it should be rolled in flour, or Indian meal, before frying, and when done brown take it up. Pour the gravy over the fish.

### 200. Chowder.

Cut some slices of pork very thin and fry it out dry in the dinner pot; then put in a layer of fish cut in slices, on the pork and fat, then a layer of onions, and then potatoes, all cut in thin slices; then fish, onions, and potatoes again, till you materials are all in, putting some salt and pepper on each layer of onions; split some crackers and dip them in water and put them around the sides and over the top; put in water enough to come up in sight; boil about half an hour, till the potatoes are done; add half a pint of milk, five minutes before you take it up.

### 201. Chowder for Invalids.

Prepare your fish and potatoes in the same way as above, omitting the pork and onions; put in equal quantities of milk and water, a little pepper, and salt.

### 202. Meat Broth.

Take from one to two pounds lean beef, veal, or mutton, and put in from three to four quarts of water, and simmer it down to two thirds the quantity : add a little rice an hour before it is done boiling. Skim the fat off when it is cold.

### 203. Chicken Broth.

May be prepared in the same way : boil till the meat is very tender.

### 204. Sago Gruel.

Two table-spoonfuls of sago to one pint of cold water, and a little salt; it will boil in a few minutes : when about done, add a little milk.

### 205. Indian Gruel.

One quart of boiling water thickened with three table spoonfuls of Indian meal, one tea-spoonful of salt; boil it and skim it till it is clear; add a little loaf sugar and nutmeg.

### 206. Preserved Peaches.

Take ripe free-stone peaches; pare, stone, and quarter them. To six pounds of the cut peaches allow three pounds of the best brown sugar.  Strew the sugar among the peaches, and set them away in a covered vessel.— Next morning put the whole into a preserving kettle, and boil it slowly about an hour and three quarters, or two hours, skimming it well.

### 207.  Preserved Raspberries.

Choose raspberries not too ripe, take the weight of them in sugar, wet the sugar with a little water, and put in the berries, let them boil softly, take care not to break them ; when clear take them up, boil the syrup until it be thick enough ; then put them in again ; do not put them away until cold.

### 208.  Preserved Quinces.

Pare and core your quince, put them into a kettle, cover them with the parings and the cores, fill up with spring water, and let them boil until they are a pink color ; take out the quinces, strain the liquor through a bag, and set it away for quince jelly ; make a syrup of loaf sugar, pound for pound, boil the quinces in it two hours, slowly, frequently putting them under the liquor ; after taking them out let the liquor boil until it is reduc· ed to a syrup.

### 209.  Preserved Tomatoes.

Take of small ripe tomatoes one peck, stick them full of holes, make a syrup of eight pounds of sugar, and put them in it, with eight lemons sliced, and two ounces of race ginger chopped fine, boil slowly three hours ; take the tomatoes out, and boil the liquor to a syrup.

### 210.  Preserved Pears.

Take six pounds of pears to four pounds of sugar, boil the parings in as much water as will cover them, strain it through a cullender, lay some pears in the bottom of your kettle, put in some sugar, and so on, alternately ; then pour the liquor off the pear skins over, boil them until they begin to look transparent, then take them out, let the juice cool, and clarify it, put the pears in again with a great deal of race ginger chopped fine, boil till done ; let the liquor boil after taking them out until it is reduced to a syrup.

### 211. Preserved Currants for Tarts.

Get your currants when they are dry, and pick them ; to every pound and a quarter of currants put a pound of sugar into a preserving pan with as much juice of currants as will dissolve it, when it boils skim it, and put in your currants aad boil them till they are clear; put them into a jar, lay paper over, tie them down, and keep them in a dry place.

### 212. Tomato Figs.

Take six pounds of sugar to one peck (or sixteen pounds) of the fruit. Scald and remove the skin of the fruit in the usual way  Cook them over a fire, their own juice being sufficient without the addition of water, until the sugar penetrates and they are clarified. They are then taken out, spread on dishes, flattened and dried in the sun. A small quantity of the syrup should be occasionally sprinkled over them whilst drying; after which, pack them down in boxes, treating each layer with powdered sugar. The syrup is afterwards concentrated and bottled for use. They keep well from year to year and retain surprisingly their flavor, which is nearly that of the best quality of fresh figs ! The pear shaped or single tomatoes answer the purpose best. Ordinary brown sugar may be used, a large portion of which is retained in syrup.

### 213. To make Currant Jelly.

Take the juice of red currants and white sugar, equal quantities in weight. Stir it gently and smoothly for three hours, put it into glasses, and in three days it will concrete into a firm jelly.

### 214. Jelly from Apples.

They are pared, quartered, and the core completly removed, and put into a pot *without* water, closely covered, and put in an oven or over a fire. When pretty well stewed, the juice is to be squeezed out through a cloth, to which a little white of an egg is added, and then the sugar. Skim it previous to boiling; then reduce it to a proper consistency, and an excellent jelly will be the product.

### 215. Tomato Sauce, for present use.

Pour boiling water on the tomatos, take the skin off, cut them up in pieces, and cover them all over with loaf sugar ; no more should be prepared than you wish to use at once, as they will not keep good.

### 216. Tomato Omelet.

When stewed, beat up half a dozen new-laid eggs, the yolk and white seperate ; when each are well beaten, mix them with the tomato — put them in a pan, and heat them up, you have a fine omelet.

### 217. To keep Apricots, Peaches, Plums, &c., fresh all the year.

Beat well together equal quantities of honey and spring water : pour it into an earthen vessel, put in the fruits all freshly gathered and cover them up quite close. When the fruit is taken out, wash it in cold water, and it is fit for immediate use.

### 218. To Dry Peaches.

The following mode of drying peaches is adopted by Thomas Belanjee, of Egg Harbour, New-Jersey :

He has a small house with a stove in it, and drawers in the sides of the house, lathed at their bottoms. Each drawer will hold nearly half a bushel of peaches, which should be ripe, and not peeled, but cut in two and laid on the laths with their skins downwards so as to save the juice. On shoving the drawer in they are soon dried by the hot air of the stove, and laid up. Peaches thus dried eat like raisins. With a paring machine, which may be had for a dollar or two, apples or pears may be pared, and a sufficient quantity dried to keep a family in pies, and apple bread and milk, till apples come again. With a paring machine, one person can pare for five or six cutters.

### 219. Peach Sauce.

Take one pint of water, one cup of sugar, wipe your peaches, clean and boil them in the water and sugar ; boil an hour. This is a delicious sauce or preserve, but will not keep good more than two or three days.

### 220. Citron Preserve.

Pare your citrons and weigh them, then scald them with a piece of allum in the water the size of a large walnut to a pailful of water, till you can pierce them with a straw — cut them in slices half an inch thick with a sharp knife, pick out the seeds, let all the pulp remain, put as much weight of sugar as there is of citron, let it stand over night, pour off the syrup, scald it, when sufficiently done put in the citron and simmer it half an hour — cool the citron and syrup separate, add mace and a sliced lemon. Some slice two or three lemons to one citron and omit the mace.

### 221. Sassafras Mead.

Mix gradually with two quarts of boiling water three and a half pounds of best brown sugar, a pint and a half of good molasses, and one fourth of a pound of *tartaric acid,* stir it well, and when cool strain it into a large jug or pan, then mix in a quarter of an ounce of essence of sassafras, transfer it to clean bottles, (it will fill about half a dozen) cork it tightly, and keep it in a cool place. Have ready a box containing about one fourth of a pound carbonate of soda, to use with it. To prepare a glass of it for drinking, pour a little of the mead into a tumbler, fill three-fourths full of cold water, then stir in a small quantity of soda and it will foam to the top. Lemon juice may be substitute, and is equally agreable.

### 222. Potatoe Yeast.

Five large potatoes boiled and mashed, three pints of boiling water, flour enough to make it a little thicker than flat jacks, and one cup of yeast. This is enough to rise five loaves of bread, which may be mixed with water, or milk, and will rise enough while you oven is heating. Save out enough of this yeast, for your next baking.

### 223. Pork Apple Pie.

Make your crust in the usual manner, spread it over a large deep plate, cut some slices of fat pork very thin, also some slices of apple; place a layer of apples, and then of pork with a very little alspice and pepper, and sugar between : three or four layers of each, with crust over the top. Bake one hour.

### 224. Ginger Beer.

One cup of ginger, one pint of molasses, one pail and a half of water, and a cup of lively yeast. Most people scald the ginger in half a pail of water, and then fill it up with a pailful of cold; but in very hot weather some people stir it up cold. Yeast must not be put in till it is cold, or nearly cold. If not to be drank within twenty four hours, it must be bottled as soon as it works.

### 225. Good wholesome Small Beer.

Take two ounces of hops, and boil them three or four hours, in three or four pailfuls of water; and then scald two quarts of molasses in the liquor, and turn it off into a clean half-barrel, boiling hot; then fill it up with cold water; before it is quite full, put in your yeast to work it; the next day you will have *agreeable wholesome Small Beer* that will not fill with wind, as that which is brewed from malt or bran; and it will keep good till it is all drank out.

### 226. Spruce Beer.

Take three gallons of water, luke warm, three half pints of molasses, a table spoonful of essence of spruce, and the same quantity of sugar; mix all together, and add a gill of yeast; let it stand over night and bottle in the morning. It will be ready to use in twenty-four hours.

### 227. Simple Remedy to Purify Water.

Pulverized alum possesses the property of purifying water. A large spoonful stirred into a hogshead of water will so purify it, that in a few hours it will be as fresh and clear as spring water. Four gallons may be purified by a tea-spoonful.

### 228. Baked Beans.

Dissolve a lump of saleratus as big as a walnut, with your beans before baking, and you will find them greatly improved.

# MEDICINAL DEPARTMENT.

---

### 229. Asthma.

When a person has an attack of this complaint, his feet should be immersed in warm *Lye Water*, or strong soap suds. Some herb tea, made of catnip or pennyroyal may be given at the same time, which will excite gentle perspiration, and will generally afford relief.

Another remedy is to beat well three eggs, including the shells, and add to them one pint of vinegar; let it stew till all is dissolved, then add one pound of loaf sugar, or one pint of molasses. Dose,—half a wine glass full to be taken occasionally, at discretion.

The fumes of burning paper, saturated with salt petre, has been known to give relief. It may be prepared by simply dipping in strong salt petre water, and then dried. On the recurrence of a turn of the asthma, a piece may be burned in the room, or rolled up and smoked by the patient.

### 230. Bleeding at the Nose.

Young persons of sanguine habits are very liable to this complaint. The internal surface of the nostrils, is lined with a net work of blood-vessels, and covered with only a thin tegument; and they are easily ruptured by any determination of more than ordinary blood to the head. Generally bleading does not continue long, but if it does, proper means should be taken to check it, by diverting the blood from the head; at such times the feet and hands will be found cold.

*Remedies.*—Soak the feet and hands in warm soap suds, or water. Apply a cloth wrung out in cold water on the back of the neck, and on the cords behind the ears.

6

Salted dried beef, grated fine with a nutmeg grater and two or three pinches snuffed up the nose it is said, will stop almost any fit of bleading.

Gum arabic, powdered fine and snuffed from your fingers, or blowed into the nose through a quill, is good.

### 231. A Remedy to stop Blood.

Soot, applied to a fresh cut or wound, will stop the blood and abate the pain at the same time.

### 232. Burns and Scalds.

Apply a poultice of Elm bark (the powdered if to be had) and milk, spread it upon a piece of linen or muslin, and when ready cover it with sweet oil ; let the poultice be changed as often as it gets dry.  If the elm bark is not at hand, scrape a potato fine and apply it.  In the absence of all other remedies, or while they are being got ready, apply cold water, by wetting soft linen or muslin cloths, and change as often as they grow warm.

*Another.*  Put as much alum in a bottle of cold water as will dissolve, and keep it ready to apply immediately to a burn.  Wet a cotton cloth in this solution, and lay it on the burn as soon as possible ; when it becomes dry or warm, wet it again ; it will ease the pain, and cure the burn in twenty-four hours, if applied before blisters are formed.  The deepest burns have been cured in this way.

Every family should have on hand, ready mixed, half a pint each, linseed oil and lime water, ready for use, in case of a burn or scald ; the bottle to be shaken previous to the application, as the ingredients will separate—lint, or a piece of linen to be applied to the burn, and kept constantly saturated with the liniment.

*Poultice.*  Indian meal poultice, covered over with young hyson tea, softened with hot water, and laid over burns and frozen flesh, as hot as it can be borne, will relieve the pain in five minutes ; if blisters have not arisen before, they will not after it is put on, and one poultice is generally sufficient to effect a cure.

*Salve.* Take a table-spoonful of lard, half a table spoonful of spirits of turpentine, and a piece of rosin as big as a walnut, and simmer them together till they are well incorporated; when cool, keep it in a box. In case of a burn, warm this so that you can spread it over a piece of linen, and apply it to the burn.

### 233. Accidents by Fire.

If females and children must wear cotton and linen dresses and aprons in the winter, use the following precaution. The dresses after being washed, should be dipped in strong alum water, which will prevent them from blazing, if they should take fire.

*Directions, in case of a person's clothes taking fire.* If a child's, or any person's clothes, should happen to be set fire to, they ought never to open the door and rush out into the street, but to lie down immediately, and if they can, to roll themselves in a rug, carpet, coat, cloak, or any other woolen article which may be near. If any other persons are present, they should assist in doing the same, as the readiest way of putting out the flame. The reason is plain. By running about through the air, you fan the flame, and make it blaze more fiercely; whereas the object should be to smother it. Do not drag the sufferer to a pump, or tear off the burnt clothes roughly; but, having extinguished the flames, remove the clothes as gently as possible, and then sprinkle flour over the burnt part of the body, the great object being to keep the air from it as much as possible. Medical direction, should, of course, be procured as quick as possible.

### 234. Cholic.

For a person afflicted with the Bilious Cholic, take the bran of corn meal, make it into a pudding, and apply it as hot as can be borne, to the bowels. It is said this will give relief.

### 235. Cancer.

Mix the yolk of an egg with fine salt, make it into a salve: spread it on a piece of soft leather, and apply it: change it every day, and a cure will soon be effected.

*Another remedy.* Use strong potash, made of the lye of the ashes of red oak bark, boiled down to the consistence of molasses, and cover the cancer with it, and in about an hour afterwards cover the plaster with tar, which must be removed after a few days, and if protuberances appear in the wound, apply more potash to them, and the plaster again until they all disappear, after which, heal the wound with any common salve. This treatment has been known to effect a perfect cure.

### 236. Cancers and Sores.

*Indian Remedy.* Take the roots of pitch pine sapplings. Chop them up fine, and boil a three pail pot full, until all the strength is exhausted, say 20 or 30 minutes; then strain off the liquor, and boil it down to one gallon, —use it as a regular drink, till a cure is effected, in one or two months. It may be sweetened with honey, molasses, or loaf sugar. This will cure Erysipelas, and other bad humors in the blood.

### 237. Consumption.

Completely to eradicate this disease, says a correspondent of the U. S. Gazette, I will not positively say the the following remedy is capable of doing; but I will venture to affirm that a temperate mode of living—avoiding spiritous liquors wholly—wearing flannel next to the skin, and taking, every morning, half a pint of new milk, mixed with a wine glass full of the compressed juice of green hoarhound, the complaint will not only be relieved, but the individual shall procure to himself a length of days beyond what its mildest form could give room to hope for.

I am myself a living witness of the beneficial effects of this agreeable, and though innocent, yet powerful application. Four weeks use of the hoarhound and milk, relieved the pains in my breast, gave me to breathe deep, long and free, strengthened and harmonized my voice, and restored me to a better state of health than I had enjoyed for years.

Dr. Coteren, of Paris, recommends the inhaling of the gaseous perfume of choloride of lime, for disease of the lungs. It may be dissolved in soft water, then pour into it a little vinegar, and apply it to the nose so as to inhale freely the perfumes which the mixture will produce.

The attention of a young lady, apparently in the last stage of consumption, was called to the virtues of camomile, by observing from her window early each morning, a dog belonging to the house, with scarcely any flesh on his bones, constantly go and lick the dew off a camomile bed in the garden, in doing which the animal was noticed to alter his appearance, to recover strength, and finally looked plump and well. The singularity of the circumstance was impressed strongly on the lady's mind, and induced her to try what effect might be produced from following the dog's example. She accordingly procured the dew from the same bed of camomile, drank a small quantity each morning, and after continuing it for some time, experienced some relief; her appetite became regular, she found a return of spirits, and in the end was completely cured.

### 238. Croup.

This disease is peculiar to children, and generally attacks them very suddenly in the night, by a very sharp, shrill cough, and quick laborious breathing, attended with a peculiar whizzing noise. At the very first notice, active measures should be pursued. Let no time be lost in giving an emetic—immerse the feet in warm water, and put a poultice of yellow snuff, mixed with goose oil, or sweet oil, upon the stomach. Apply several thicknesses of flannel wet in hot water over the throat, as hot as can be borne, and change as often as it cools. Put onion poultices on the feet, after soaking them a little time.

### 239. Corns.

Soak the feet in warm soap suds, till the outer surface of the corn is quite soft : then wipe dry and apply caustic all over the corn; it will soon be dry; let them remain for several days till you can remove the black skin without difficulty, then apply more caustic, and so continue till there is no corn left.

6*

*Another remedy.* Take a small piece of flannel which has not been washed, wrap or sew it round the corn and toe. One thickness will be sufficient. Wet the flannel where the corn is, night and morning, with fine sweet oil. Renew the flannel weekly, and at the same time, pare the corn, which will very soon disappear.

It is said that a piece of tobacco, moistened, and bound upon a corn, acts as an effectual cure.

### 240. Coughs.

In hard, unyielding coughs, the following recipe will be useful : One gill of molasses, one do. N. Rum, two tea spoonfuls of pulverized liquorice, and a piece of alum as large as a walnut.

### 241. Whooping Cough.

This complaint is mostly confined to children, and will have a regular run. A little saleratus, and occasionally a little blood root, will be found greatly to alleviate the paroxysms.

### 242. Chilblains.

Take one part muriatic acid, mingled with seven parts water, with which the feet must be well rubbed for a night or two before going to bed, and perfect relief will be experienced. The application must of course be made before the skin breaks, and it will be found not only to allay the itching, but to prevent the further progress of the chilblains.

*Another good remedy,* is to dip the feet every night and morning in cold water, withdrawing them in a minute or two, and drying them with a hard coarse towel. If the feet are frosted, put them in a pail of brine.

### 243. Chapped Hands.

Wash your hands with Castile soap—apply it with a flannel, and, if necessary, use a brush, in order to get the dirt from under and around the nails and fingers, till they are perfectly clean, then rinse them in a little clean water, and while they are wet, *rub them well all over* with about half a tea-spoonful of good honey; then *dry them well*, with a clean coarse towel. This should be done once or twice a day, and always before going to bed.

### 244. Castor Oil;

*To make it palatable to children.*

Take the quantity of oil you propose for a dose, and boil it for a few minutes in an equal quantity of milk, and sweeten it with a little sugar : when cool, stir it, and give it to the child. The taste is quite pleasant, and not disagreeable.

### 245. Dysentery.

Take two wine glasses each, sweet oil, good molasses, and West India Rum, and simmer them well together over a fire till it becomes the thickness of honey, so that the oil will not separate from the rest; while on the fire keep it well stirred, and when taken off, continue the same till it is cold. A grown person should take a table spoonful once an hour, till he finds the disease abating, then once in two hours, or as the judgment may suggest. Children to take in like manner, in proportion to their ages.

Boiled milk, thickened with flour, and taken in the first stages of dysentery, is in all common cases an invaluable remedy. Boiled milk without flour is too harsh.

A table spoonful of powdered charcoal, mixed with a little water, if taken in time, will check the dysentery.

Take the yolks of three eggs, two ounces of loaf sugar, one gill of brandy, and one nutmeg grated ; the whole to be well mixed. A grown person to take a tea-spoonful every two or three hours; children less, according to age. This is said to be an excellent remedy for the dysentery.

### 246. Diarrhea.

To a wine glass of warm water, add one table spoonful of vinegar, and one tea-spoonful of fine salt. Take this at one dose, and if it does not afford relief in half an

hour, repeat the dose.  The second dose is almost sure
to give entire relief.  This is said also to give relief in
case of Bilious Cholic.

Another remedy more adapted to children, is to parch
half a pint of rice until it is perfectly brown, then boil it
down as is usually done, and eat it slowly, and it will
stop very bad diarrhea in a few hours.

### 247. Dropsy.

Take two handfuls of the green or inner bark of the
white common elder, steep it in two quarts of white
Lisbon wine twenty-four hours ; take a gill of the wine in
the morning, fasting, or more if it can be borne; or if
more convenient, in the morning, and part about noon,
on an empty stomach.

Common dandelion is also said to be very good in cases
of Dropsy.  It may be eaten as a salad with the usual
dressing, or the juice may be taken in the dose of half a
wine glass full, three times a day—or the leaves may be
kept in the pocket, and frequently eaten in the course of
the day.  The afflicted will rest satisfied with the change
of their feelings, which will be perceived after using the
plant.

### 248. Deafness.

Take a strong glass bottle and fill it nearly full of
pure clarified honey, insert the bottle into the center of
a loaf of unbaked bread, first taking care to stop it tightly, and bake the whole thoroughly in an oven.  Pour a
small quantity of the honey thus treated into your ears,
and protect them from the action of the external air by
the use of cotton.

### 249. Drowning.

The following directions are given by Valentine Mott,
Surgeon General of the American Shipwreck Society, in
New York :

*To bring the Drowned to Life.*

Immediately, as soon as the body is removed from the
water, press the chest suddenly and forcibly *downward
and backward*, and *instantly* discontinue the pressure.

Repeat this *without interruption*, until a pair of common bellows can be procured. When obtained, introduce the nozzle well upon the *base of the tongue.* Surround the mouth with a towel or handkerchief and close it. Direct a bystander to press firmly upon the projecting part of the neck (called Adam's apple) *and use the bellows actively.* Then press upon the chest to expel the air from the lungs, to imitate natural breathing. Continue this, *at least an hour*, unless signs of natural breathing come on.

Wrap the body in blankets, place it near a fire, and do every thing to preserve the natural warmth, as well as to impart an artificial heat, if possible. *Every thing, however, is secondary to inflating the lungs.* ☞ *Send for a medical man immediately.*

*Avoid all frictions until respiration shall be in some degree restored.*

### 250. Inflamed Eyes.

Pour boiling water on elder flowers, and steep them ; when cold, put three or four drops of laudanum into a small glass of the tea, and let the mixture run into the eyes several times a day. They will become strong in a few days.

### 251. To remove a Mote from the Eye.

Take a horse hair, and form a loop by bending it round and bringing the ends together, then raise the eye-lid, and insert the loop between the lid and the eye-ball, then let the lids fall again, draw the hair out, and with it whatever may have got under the lid.

### 252. Elderberry Syrup.

Take of the juice of elderberry one quart ; boil to one pint ; strain, and add two pounds double refined sugar ; again place it over the fire ; as soon as it shall have boiled, remove it from the fire ; and when cold, bottle it for use, taking care to have it well corked. Should you neglect to put in the above quantity of sugar, there will be danger of its becoming mouldy. As a gentle purgative, this syrup is an excellent medicine, of very pleasant taste, and is particularly servicable for children who are difficult about taking medicine.  The dose for an adult is a wine glass full.

### 253.  Elixir Asthmatic

Take opium, one drachm ; oil of aunice, one drachm ; gum camphor, two-thirds of a drachm ; extract of liquorice one ounce ; three gills of alcohol, and three gills of water : put the materials in a bottle with the alcohol and let it stand three days before adding the water.  Age improves this very much.

### 254.  Ear-Ache.

Soak the feet in warm water ; roast an onion and put the heart of it into the ear  as warm as can be borne ; heat a brick and  wrap it up and  apply it to the side of the head.  When the feet are taken from the water, bind roasted onions on them.

### 255.  Felons.

Soak the part in weak lye, (which can easily be made of a small piece of potash,) as hot as you can bear it, for twenty or thirty minutes ; shave down the skin on the part, but don't make it bleed ; then take a piece of clay, dry, pulverize and sift it, moisten it with strong camphor to the consistency of a poultice ; apply it half an inch thick, and keep it moist with camphor, as much as it will absorb, for a day or two.  This is said to be a sure cure, without disfiguring the part affected.

### 256.  Gravel.

Lime water, about a gill at a time, as a drink, and repeated often, is good in this disease.  The warm bath should be used, and flannel rung out of a decoction of warm herbs, should be kept on the bowels.  Drink moderate draughts of gum arabic, warm.  When the pain subsides, use gentle physic.

A correspondent says he was relieved of this complaint of a number of years standing, by sweetening his tea with half honey and half sugar.

### 257.  Hydrophobia.

Take oyster shells, wash them clean, put them upon a bed of live coals, and keep them there till they are thoroughly calcined, or burnt; then reduce them to fine powder, and sift it through a fine seive. Take three table spoonfuls of this powder, or lime, and add a sufficiency of egg to give it the consistency of soft dough,—fry it in a little fresh butter or olive oil. Let the patient eat this cake in the morning, and abstain from food or drink, at least six hours. This dose repeated for three mornings in succession, is, in all cases, sufficient.

A gentleman states that he is acquainted with six persons who were bitten from eight to fifteen years ago, by dogs who were abundantly proved to be mad, from the fact that animals bitten immediately after died with every symptom of hydrophobia; but by the use of this remedy, are yet in perfect health.

### 258. Hair Restorative.

It is stated in the Medical Journal, that a gentleman whose head was quite bald, had his hair entirely restored by the use of sulphate of copper dissolved in brandy and applied to his head.

Fine salt dissolved in water, and daily applied, it is said will restore hair to the heads of those who, from fever or other causes, may have suffered its loss.

### 259. Remedy for Indigestion.

Boil half-a-pint of white wheat three hours in a quart of water, or little more if necessary. Drink half-a-pint of the liquid twice or three times a week.

### 260. Opedeldoc.

Take an ounce of gum camphor, half a drachm oil of rosemary, half a drachm of oil of origanum, two ounces castile soap, cut small, and half a pint spirits of wine. Boil all together for half an hour. When cool, bottle it for use. It is good for bruises, sprains, stiffness of the neck and shoulders, and rheumatic pains.

### 291. Pile Ointment.

Take excrescences which form upon the leaves of the sumac, very finely powdered, an ounce; fresh lard, six ounces. Blend them together thoroughly. This is beneficial in piles, and often affords surprising relief. It may be confined to the parts, by means of a bandage and a-piece of lint or folded rag.

Burdock leaves, applied all round the parts and back, is good.

### 262. Injection for Piles.

If the parts are very sore or irritable, the injection may consist of an infusion of raspberry, witch-hazel, or sumac leaves, rendered somewhat mucilaginous with slippery elm; and as soon as it can be borne, ginger, cayenne, or rheumatic drops may be added. The liquid should always be strained, or the sediment will tend to aggravate the complaint.

### 263. Pile Electuary.

Take cream of tartar, one ounce; jalap pulverized, one ounce; electuary of senna, two ounces; flour of sulphur half an ounce; nitrate of potash, half an ounce; add molasses sufficient to make a pill, or thick mass; make into pills of common size, and take four night and morning. This is a sovereign remedy for blind or bleeding piles. Sometimes when the tumors become very painful, and are attended with considerable inflammation, a poultice of slippery elm bark and milk will be found quite valuable and soothing.

### 264. Run Round on the Finger.

As soon as the swelling and inflammation begins, lay the finger flat on the table, and scratch the nail all over, first lengthways and then crossways, with the sharp point of scissors or penknife, so as to scratch up the whole surface of the nail, leaving it rough and white. This latter operation will not give the slightest pain, and we have never known it to fail of stopping the progress of the disease, all symptoms of which will disappear by the next day.

### 265. Rheumatism.

Take one quart of spirits of wine, two ounces of laudanum, one ounce oil of ambre, one ounce oil of pennyroyal, one ounce spirits of hartshorn; mix the ingredients in a glass bottle : rub the parts several times by the fire, then cover them with flannel. Keep it well corked from the air, to prevent evaporation. This is excellent for fresh cuts, sprains, and bruises.

Half an ounce of saltpetre dissolved in a pint of brandy, and taken one table spoonful every day. This is said by those who have tried the experiment, to be a most excellent antidote for that painful complaint.

### 266. Ring Worm.

Put some tobacco with some water, and boil it, and add some vinegar and strong lye to the liquor : wash the parts affected often.

### 267. Sore Throat.

Mix a wine-glass full of good calcined magnesia and honey to the consistence of paste or jelly, and take a spoonful once an hour through the day for a day or two. It is *cooling*, *healing*, and a very gentle *cathartic*.

*External Remedy.* Take a glass of olive or sweet oil, and half a glass of spirits of turpentine; mix them together, and rub the throat externally, wearing flannel round it at the same time. It proves most effectual when applied early.

### 268. Tooth Ache.

Mix alum and common salt in equal quantities, finely pulverized. Then wet some cotton, large enough to fill the cavity, which cover with salt and alumn and apply it. We have the authority of those who have tested it, to say it will prove a perfect remedy.

The bark of wild poplar root steeped in water, and the liquid held in the mouth, it is said will cure the tooth ache.

For the ague, put as much cotton in the mouth as can conveniently be kept in, and in a few hours the pain and inflammation will be gone. If the swollen part of the face is covered with cotton, the swelling will soon disappear.

7

### 269. Tooth Wash.

To four ounces of fresh prepared lime-water add a drachm of peruvian bark ; wash the teeth with this water before breakfast, and after supper ; it will effectually destroy the tartar and remove the offensive smell from those which are decayed.

### 270. Warts.

Dissolve as much common washing soda as the water will take up—then wash the hands or warts with this for a minute or two, and allow them to dry without being wiped. This repeated for two or three days, will gradually destroy the most irritable wart.

The bark of willow burnt to ashes, mixed with good vinegar, and applied to warts, it is said will remove them.

### 271. To Stop Vomiting.

Pound up gum camphor, pour on boiling water ; sweeten it with loaf sugar, and let the patient take a spoonful every ten minutes. A drink made of common pig weed, is also said to be a good remedy. Also, a mustard poultice applied to the pit of the stomach, is good.

### 272. Gravel or Stone.

Take a large handful of arse-smart : make a decoction, and add one gill of gin, and take the whole in twelve hours. This has been known to discharge a table spoonful of gravel stones at a time.

### 273. Nightmare.

Stick a needle or pin in the night shirt so that the point of it will touch the skin upon the breast, thereby keeping up a sense of feeling in the part ; and when this is effected, the nightmare is prevented.

### 274. Dysentery.

Take one tea-spoonful rhubarb, pulverized ; one do. peppermint leaves, pulverized ; one do. saleratus ; half pint boiling water ; when cold, add a wine glass of brandy, and sweeten with loaf sugar. *Dose*—half a wine glass full once in two or three hours, till the disease is checked.

# MISCELLANEOUS RECEIPTS.

275. *To keep Apples for Winter use.* Put them in casks or bins, in layers well covered with dry sand, each layer being covered. This preserves them from the air, from moisture, and from frost; it prevents their perishing by their own perspiration, their moisture being absorbed by the sand; at the same time it preserves the flavor of the apples, and prevents their wilting. Pippins have been kept in this manner sound and fresh till midsummer; and how much longer they would have kept is not known. Any kind of sand will answer, but it must be perfectly dry.

276. *Liquid Blacking.* Take eight ounces of ivory black, six ounces of molasses, six table spoonfuls of sweet oil, and three of oil of vitrol: mix all together with a quart of vinegar, and bottle it. It will be ready for use in a week.

277. *Another.* Take elder-berries, mash them in a kettle of water, place the kettle for a few days in the shade until the liquid ferments, then boil it for half a day, filling up with water occasionally: set it aside to cool, then strain it through a coarse thin cloth, then boil it down to the thickness of molasses, and it is fit for use. Put a small quantity on a brush with a feather and rub the shoe until you bring it to a fine gloss. Good writing ink may be made in the same way.

278. *To make Boots water proof.* Put a pound of tallow and half a pound of rosin into a pot on the fire; when melted and mixed, warm the boots, and apply the hot stuff with a painter's brush, until neither the sole nor upper leather will suck in any more. If it is desired that the boots should immediately take a polish, dissolve an ounce of bees' wax in an ounce of spirits of turpentine,

7*

to which add a tea-spoonful of lampblack. A day or two after the boots have been treated with tallow and rosin, rub over them the wax in turpentine, but not before the fire. Thus the exterior will have a coat of wax alone, and shine like a mirror. Boots or shoes should be so large as to admit of wearing in them cork soles. Cork is so bad a conductor of heat, that, with it in the boot, the feet are always warm on the coldest stone floor.

279. *Cheap Bed of Husks.* In Spain and Portugal, beds are made of the husks of corn, which are very durable, convenient, and healthy. These beds are made in the following manner :—The husks are gathered as soon as they are ripe, and on a clean dry day. The outer husks are rejected, and the softer, inner ones, are collected and dried in the shade, and when dry, the hard ends that were attached to the cob are cut off. They are then drawn through a hatchel or comb, so as to cut them into narrow slips. These, enclosed in a sack, or formed into a matress like prepared hair, will be found almost equal to the best moss or hair matresses, and are so durable, that with any ordinary care, they will last from five to ten years.

280. *Good Butter in Winter.* Before setting the milk, pour a sufficient quantity of boiling water into it to make it nearly as hot as it can be borne by the finger. Keep the cream from freezing, and when it is ready to churn, add the juice of a middling sized carrot to four quarts of cream.

281. *Cologne Water.* Take two drachms of oil of rosemary, two of the oil of lemon, one of lavender, ten of cinnamon, one tea-spoonful of rose water. Pour on these one quart of alcohol ; put all in a glass bottle, and shake it up well. To have it very clear, put some cotton in a tunnel, and place a piece of clean tissue or printing paper over it, and strain the contents through it.

282. *Another way.* 1 pint alcohol, 60 drops lavender, 60 do. bergamot, 60 do. essence of lemon, 60 do. orange water. To be corked up, and well shaken. It is better for considerable age.

283. *Choloride of Lime.* To correct the most impure and offensive atmosphere, in a few moments, and to

restore it to its purity, it is only necessary to procure one pound of choloride of lime, which will cost but one shilling, put it into a bucket of water, mix it up, and throw it into a receptacle of filth. A supply may be had at almost any of the apothecaries.

284. *To preserve Corn for Boiling.* Pluck the corn when fit for eating, strip down the husk so as to remove the silk, and then replace it—pack it away in a barrel, and pour on a strong pickle, such as used for meat, with a weight to keep it down, and you will have a good sea stock—par-boiled and then boiled to make it perfectly fresh and sweet as when taken from the salt.

285. *To remove Flies from Rooms.* Take half a tea-spoonful of black pepper, in powder, one tea-spoonful of brown sugar, and one table spoonful of cream ; mix them well together, and place them in a room on a plate where the flies are troublesome, and they will soon disappear.

286. *To prevent Horses being teased by flies.* Take two or three small handfuls of walnut leaves, upon which pour two or three quarts of cold water ; let it infuse one night, and pour the whole, next morning, into a kettle, and boil for quarter of an hour ; when cold, it is fit for use. Moisten a sponge with it, and before the horse goes out of the stable, let those parts which are most irritable be smeared over with liquor. Pennyroyal prepared in the same way, is equally good. Flies will not alight a moment on the spot to which this has been applied.

287. *A cheap method of preserving Cucumber Plants from the small fly or bug.* Break off the stocks of the onions which have been set out in the spring, and stick down five or six of them in each hill of cucumbers, and the bug will immediately leave them. It would be well, after a few days, to renew them ; but one application has frequently been found to be completely effectual.

288. *To extract grease with Camphine Oil.* Grease of the very worse sort (for instance whale oil,) may be extracted immediately, even from silks, ribbons, and other delicate articles, by means of camphine oil, which can always be procured from the lamp-shops. As this

oil is the better for being fresh, get but a small quantity at a time.  Pour some camphine into a clean cup, and dip lightly into it a bit of clean, soft, white rag.  With this rub the grease spot.  Then take a fresh rag dipped in the camphine, and continue rubbing till the grease is extracted, which will be very soon.  You will find the color of the article uninjured.  To remove the turpentine odor of the camphine, rub the place with cologne-water or strong spirits of wine, and expose it to the open air. If any of the camphine scent remains, repeat the cologne. We have known whale oil grease removed from white satin by this process.

For a carpet or any article of furniture that cannot be immediately exposed to the open air, it is best to remove grease spots by the application of scraped Wilmington clay ; or by covering the place with buckwheat batter, left on all day, and renewed in the evening or next morning.

**289.**  *To take Ink out of linen.*  Dip the spotted part in pure melted tallow ; then wash out the tallow, and the ink will come out with it.  This is said to be unfailing.

**290.**  *Scratches in Horses.*  Mix white lead and linseed oil in such proportions as will render the application convenient, and I never have known more than two or three applications necessary to effect a common cure.

**291.**  *How to fatten Fowls.*  Confine your fowls in a large airy inclosure, and feed them on broken Indian corn, Indian meal, or mush, with raw potatoes, cut into small pieces, not larger than a filbert, placing within their reach a quantity of charcoal broken into small pieces.

**292.**  *To make good Black Ink.*  Rasped logwood, one ounce ; nutgall, three ounces ; gum arabic, two ounces ; sulphate of iron, (green copperas) one ounce ; rain water, two quarts.  Boil the water and wood together until the liquid is reduced one half ; then add the nutgalls coarsely bruised, and when nearly cold the sulphate of iron and gum ;  stir it frequently for a few days, then let it settle—then pour it off and cork it up close in a glass bottle.

**293.**  *Indelible Ink.*  Take six cents worth of Lunar

caustic, and having put it into an ounce phial full of vinegar, cork it tight and hang in the sun. In a couple of days it will be fit for use.

To make the preparation for the above, take a lump of pearlash, of the size of a chesnut, and dissolve it in a gill of rain water.

The part of the muslin to be written upon is to be wet with the preparation, and dried and glazed with a warm flat iron; immediately after which it is ready for marking.

294. *To keep up Sash Windows.* This is performed by means of cork, in the simplest manner and without scarcely any expense. Bore three or four holes in the sides of the sash, into which insert common bottle corks, projecting about the sixteenth part of an inch. These will press against the window frames, along the usual groove, and by their elasticity support the sash at any height which may be required.

295. *To escape from, or go into a house on fire.*— Creep or crawl with your face near the ground, and although the room be full of smoke to suffocation, yet near the floor the air is pure, and may be breathed with safety. The best escape from upper windows is a knotted rope, but if a leap is unavoidable, then a bed should be thrown out first, or beds prepared for the purpose.

296. *Fire-escape.* In nurseries, and in other rooms where little children sleep, there ought to be provided one or more strong sacks, about three feet and a half in depth, and one and a half in diameter, kept open at the top with a thick wooden hoop, having a long rope fastened to it : into these sacks, should an unhappy accident require it, the children may be put, and let down. The person who manages the above, may descend by the same fire-escape fastened to the bedstead, or such other means as may be at hand.

297. *To extinguish a recent fire.* A mop and a pail of water are generally the most efficacious remedies ; but if it has gained head then keep out the air, and remove all ascending or perpendicular combustibles, up which the fire creeps and increases in force as it rises.

7**

298.  *To extinguish fire in chimnies.*  Put a wet blanket over the whole front of the fire-place, which soon stops the current of air, and extinguishes the flame.

299.  *To take ink out of linen.*  Take a piece of mould candle, (or common candle will do nearly as well,) melt it, and dip the spotted part of the linen into the melted tallow.  It may then be washed, and the spots will disappear without injuring the linen.  This is the best method hitherto discovered.

300.  *To take out pitch, tar, rosin, &c.*  If any of these happen to get on a garment, either linen or woolen, pour a little spirits of turpentine on the place, and let it soak in about half an hour.  Then rub it gently, and you will find the turpentine has soaked out the glutinous quality, so that it will easily crumble out.

301.  *To preserve and waterprove boots and shoes.*— Simmer over a slow fire, till well mixed, a quarter of a pound of mutton suet cut into small pieces, a quarter of a pint of linseed oil, and two ounces of rosin in powder, and with a small painter's tool brush lay it over the shoes or boots whilst warm, and if they are well blacked before the process they will take the blacking almost immediately afterwards.  This renders them water-proof, and makes them last much longer.

302.  *A strong cement for china or glass.*  With a small camel-hair brush rub the broken edges with a little carriage oil varnish ; and if neatly put together the fracture will hardly be perceptible, and when thoroughly dry will stand both fire and water.

303.  *To preserve beef for a year.*  For 100 lbs. preserve the following : 4 quarts coarse salt, made fine ; 4 lbs. brown sugar ; 2 oz. saltpetre.  Mix the articles well together, then rub your meat with it, and pack it closely in the barrel ; sufficient pickle will soon be made in the barrel by this process.  By no means use any water, as it will spoil the meat when the weather becomes warm. If, at any time, a scum rise on the barrel, skim it off and sprinkle into it a little fine salt, which will preserve the pickle.  Never take the pickle out to boil it.  This will harden the beef and change its flavor.

**304.** *Tainted Beef.* Salted beef that has begun to taint may be restored to its original sweetness by taking it out of the pickle and packing it over again in layers of charcoal ; after which a new and sweet pickle, with a little saltpetre added, should be poured on it. The charcoal, it is said, will take out all taste of taint in a week.

**305.** *To make Vinegar.* Boil slowly for one hour, three pounds of very coarse brown sugar in three gallons of water, work it with a little yeast, the same as you would beer, then put it into a cask, and expose it to the sun, with a piece of brown paper pasted over the bunghole ; and it will soon become fine vinegar, fit for pickling or any other purpose.

**306.** *To take grease spots out of silk or woolen cloth.* Dip a piece of clean flannel into spirits of turpentine, and rub the spots until they disappear, which will not be long,

**307.** *To preserve Apples.* If apples are immersed in grain of any kind, they will keep good all the year round, and the grain will not in any way be the worse for it. This does not need any preparation or expense, as the apples may be put into a corn-bin or into a tub, and the corn intended for food for horses or poultry may as well be stored in this way as any other.

**308.** *To preserve Eggs.* If you take the eggs as soon as the hen has laid them, and smear the shells with lard or butter, they will keep as good as new laid eggs for some time ; but if you rub the shells with butter at any time, it will keep them good for months, and will prevent their being hatched.

**309.** *Cold starch for linen.* There is economy in stiffening the collars and wristbands of shirts with unboiled starch. Take as much of the best raw starch as will fill half a common tumbler, or a half pint cup. Fill it nearly up with very clear cold water. Mix it well with a spoon, pressing out all the lumps, till you get it thoroughly dissolved. Next add a tea-spoonful of salt to prevent its sticking. Pour it into a broad earthen pan, and add gradually a pint of clear cold water, and stir and mix it well. Do not boil it.

The shirts having been washed and dried, dip the

wristbands into this starch, and then squeeze it out. Between each dipping, stir it up from the bottom with a spoon. Then sprinkle the shirts, and fold or roll them up with the collars and wristbands folded evenly, inside. They will be ready to iron in an hour.

This quantity of cold starch is sufficient for the collars and wristbands of a dozen shirts. Ladies' collars may be done also with cold starch, if the muslin is not very thin.

310. *To boil potatoes mealy.* Select them of a uniform size, and pour over them cold water in an uncovered pot just sufficient to cover them. When this first water nearly boils, pour it off, and replace it with a similar quantity of salted cold water. They will thus be mealy and not cracked. The prongs of a fork will prove when they are done.

311. *To make patent liquid blacking.* To two ounces of ivory black, add one tea-spoonful of oil of vitrol, one table spoonful of sweet oil, and two ounces of brown sugar; roll the same into a ball, and to dissolve it add half a pint of vinegar.

312. *Musquitoes.* Attach a piece of flannel or sponge to a thread, made fast to the top of the bedstead, wet the flannel or sponge with camphorated spirits, and the Musquitoes will leave the room.

313. *Smelling Salts.* Subcarbonate of ammonia, 8 parts. Put it in coarse powder into a bottle, and pour on it Oil of lavender, 1 part.

314. *To prevent the smoking of a lamp.* Soak the wick in strong vinegar, and dry it well before you use it; it will then burn both sweet and pleasant, and give much satisfaction for the trifling trouble in preparing it.

315. *Cuts.* In case of a common cut, bind the lips of the wound together with a rag and put nothing else on. If the cut be large, and so situated that it cannot be bound up, use sticking plaster cut in stripes and laid obliquely across the cut. If necessary, take a stitch or two with a needle and thread on each lip of the wound, and draw the two sides together.

If an artery be cut, it must be immediately tied up or the person will bleed to death. The blood from an artetery is of a bright red color, and spirts out, in regular jits, at each beat of the heart. Take up the bleeding end of the artery, and hold it, or tie it up, till a surgeon arrives. When the artery cannot be found, and in all cases of bad cuts on any of the limbs, apply compression; when it can be done, tie a very tight bandage *above* the wound, if it be below the heart, and *below*, if the wound be above the heart. Put a stick into the band and twist it as tight as can be borne till surgical aid can be obtained.

316. *Blow on the head.* In case of a blow on the head, or a fall causing insensibility, use a mustard paste on the back of the neck and pit of the stomach, and rub the body with spirits. After the circulation is restored, bleeding is often necessary; but it is very dangerous to attempt it before.

317. *Frozen Pumps.* Nothing is more discouraging in a cold winter morning, when the thermometer is 10 or 15 degrees below zero, than to find your pump handle immovable, and be obliged to spend all the forenoon before you can water your cattle, or have any water from this source for family purposes. A careful housekeeper will always in this weather keep a pailful in a place where it will not freeze. If your pump is copper or any kind of metal, all you have to do is to take your teakettle from the fire, and pour some boiling water on the outside of the pump and pipe as far as it is frozen, and you will find immediate relief.

318. *A brilliant Stucco Whitewash.* Six quarts of clean lime, slacked in boiling water, 2 quarts of salt, 5 gallons of water : boil and skim, then add one pound of copperas, and 3-4 pound of pearlash, gradually, and four quarts sifted wood ashes; color to taste or fancy; applied while hot.

2d. Clean, fresh-burnt lime, same as above; 1-4 lb. burnt alum, powdered; 1 lb. sugar; 3 pints rice flour, made into a jelly; 1 lb. clean glue, first dissolved; 5 gallons water.

This wash is applied where particular neatness is required, with a painter's brush. It must be put on while warm, if upon the outside of the building—if within doors, cold. It will retain its brilliancy for many years. There is nothing of the kind that will compare with it. About one pint of this mixture will cover a square yard upon the outside of a house, if properly applied.

319. *Red Ants*—to keep them away from your cupboards. Keep some tar water in an earthern vessel in your closets, and you will not be troubled with little red ants.

320. *Method of preserving grapes.* Take a cask or barrel, inaccessible to the external air, and put into it a layer of bran, dried in an oven, or of ashes well dried and sifted. Upon this, place a layer of grapes well cleaned, and gathered in the afternoon of a dry day, before they are perfectly ripe. Proceed thus with alternate layers of bran and grapes, till the barrel is full, taking care that the grapes do not touch each other, and to let the last layer be of bran ; then close the barrel, so that the air may not be able to penetrate, which is an essential point. Grapes thus packed, will keep nine or even twelve months.

321. *To clean the teeth.* Take of good soft water, one quart ; juice of lemon, two ounces ; burnt alum, six grains ; common salt, six grains. Mix. Boil them a minute in a cup, then strain and bottle for use.

322. *Hic-cough.* It is said that this very unpleasant sensation may be instantly stopped by taking a tea-spoonful of vinegar, or a few draughts of cold water in succession. Peppermint water, mixed with a few drops of vitroil in acid, will stop it.

323. *To mend iron pots.* To repair cracks, &c., in iron pots or pans, mix some finely sifted lime with well beaten whites of eggs, till reduced to a paste, then add some iron file dust, and apply the composition to the injured part, and it will soon become hard and fit for use.

324. *Potato Starch.* Peel and grate a quantity of potatoes ; put the pulp into a coarse cloth between two boards, and press it into a dry cake ; the juice thus pressed out of the potato, must be mixed with an equal quantity of water, and in an hour's time it will deposite a fine sediment, which may be used as starch.

325. *To raise the surface of velvet.* Warm a flat iron moderately; cover it with a wet cloth, and hold it under the velvet; the vapor arising from the heated cloth will raise the pile of the velvet with the assistance of a rush-whisk.

326. *To prevent flies injuring picture frames, glasses, &c.* Boil three or four leeks in a pint of water, then with a gilding brush do over your glasses and frames, and the flies will not alight on the article so washed. This may be used without apprehension, as it will not do the least injury to the frames.

327. *A hint to the working classes.* If a man 21 years of age, begin to save a dollar a week, and put it to interest every year, he would have at 31 years of age, six hundred and fifty dollars; at 41, one thousand six hundred and eighty; at 61, six thousand one hundred and fifty; and at 71, eleven thousand five hundred dollars. When we look at these sums, and when we think how much temptation and evil might be avoided in the very act of saving them, and how much good a man in humble circumstances might do for his family by these sums, we cannot help wondering that there are not more savers of $1 a week.

328. *Jefferson's two rules.* Two rules of Jefferson are very applicable to the times :—" Never spend your money before you get it ;" and " Never buy what you do not want because it is cheap."

329. *The Tool Closet.* Much inconvenience and considerable expense would be saved, if it was the universal custom to keep in every house a few tools for the purpose of performing at home what are called small jobs ; instead of being always obliged to send for a mechanic and pay him for executing little things, that might be sufficiently well done by a man or boy belonging to the family—provided that the proper instruments were at hand. The cost of these articles is very trifling, and the advantages of having them in the house, (particularly in the country,) are beyond all price. In a small private family it may not be necessary to keep more than a few of these things; but that few are almost indispensible to

comfort. For instance, there should be an axe, a saw, (a wood-saw also, where wood is burnt,) a claw-hammer, a mallet, a gimblet, a screw-driver, a small plane, a carpet-fork or stretcher, one or two jack-knives, a pair of large scissors or sheers, and a trowel. If there were two gimblets and two screw-drivers (large and small,) it would be better still. Also an assortment of hooks and nails of different sizes, from large spikes down to small tacks, not forgetting a portion of brass-headed nails, some large and some smaller. Screws also will be found very convenient. The nails and screws should be kept in a wooden box with divisions or partitions to separate the various sorts, for it is very troublesome to have them mixed.

No house should be without glue, chalk, putty, paint, cord, twine, and wrapping paper; and care should be taken that the supply is not suffered to run out, lest the deficiency might cause delay and inconvenience at a time when most wanted.

It is well to have in the lower part of the house a deep closet, appropriated entirely to tools and things of equal utility, for executing at once such little repairs as convenience may require, without the delay or expense of sending for an artisan. This closet should have only one large shelf, and that not more than three feet above the floor. Beneath the shelf may be a deep drawer divided in two. This drawer may contain cakes of glue, pieces of chalk, hanks of manilla-grass cord, and balls of twine of different size and quality. There may be small shelves at the sides of the closet for glue-pots, paste-pots, and brushes ; pots for black, white, green, and red paint, cans of painting oil, &c. On the wall above the large shelf let the tools be suspended, or laid across nails or hooks of proper size to support them. This is much better than to keep them in a box, where they may be injured by rubbing against each other, and the hand may be hurt by feeling among them to find the one that is wanted. When hung against the closet-wall each tool may be seen at a glance. We have been shown an excellent and simple contrivance for designating the exact places of these things. On the wall directly under the nails that support the tools is drawn, with a small brush dipped in black paint or ink, an outline representation of the tool or instrument appropriated to that particular place. For instance, under each saw is sketched the outline of a saw ; under each gimlet is a sketch of a gimlet ; under the screw-drivers are slight drawings of screw drivers. So that when any tool is taken away for use, and afterwards brought back again, the exact spot to which it belongs may be found in a moment ; and all confusion in putting them up and finding them again is thus prevented. We highly recommend this plan.

Wrapping paper may be piled on the floor under the large shelf. It can be bought very low by the ream, at the wholesale paper stores ; and each house should be supplied with it—in several varieties. For instance, coarse brownish paper for common things. That denominated iron-monger's paper, which is strong, thick, and in large sheets, is useful for inclosing heavy articles. Nankeen paper is best for putting up nice parcels, such as books, and things of fine quality. What is called shoe-paper, (each ream containing a variety of colors, red, blue, white and buff,) is very useful also for wrapping nice articles, as it is soft and not brittle. This paper is cheapest of all.

Old waste newspapers are unfit for wrapping any other articles than glass, china, brass, and tin—things whose surfaces are so hard and polished that the printing-ink does not rub off on them—also they can be easily washed. Waste newspapers had best be used for lighting fires, singeing poultry, and cleaning windows and mirrors. Waste written paper is of little use but for allumettes or lamp-lighters. It is well to keep a large jar or bag to receive scraps of old paper, as it sells for a cent a pound ; and these cents may be given to a poor person.

We have seen people, when preparing for a journey, or putting up things to send away, " at their wit's end" for want of a sheet of good wrapping paper, a string of twine, a few nails, or a little paint to mark a box. We have seen a door kept open during the whole of a cold day and a cold night, for want of a screw-driver to fix a disordered lock. It seems scarcely credible that any respectable house should be without a hammer—yet we have known persons whose sole dependence for that indispensable article, was on borrowing of a neighbor. And when the hammer was obtained, there were perhaps no nails in the house of the size that was wanted.

The attention of boys should be early directed to the

use of common tools. And, if they had tools at hand, there are few boys in our country that would not take pleasure in using them. By seeing carpenters, glaziers, locksmiths, and bell hangers at work, they may very soon learn to be passably expert in these arts; and frequently a smart and observant boy will acquire great amateur proficiency in them. In a house, where among other tools, there was always a glazier's diamond, knife, &c., we have seen a pane of glass put into a broken window as neatly as if done by a professor of the art.

We have known boys who could make a box or a bench, or a little table; who could hang and repair bell-wires, mend locks and hinges, paper or paint a small room, mend a broken window cord, re-lay a brick hearth, repair the yard pavement; and find great amusement in doing these things.

We once knew a family of four boys living in Philadelphia, who entirely, and with their own hands, built for themselves in a large yard, what they called a play-house; that is a house to play in when the weather was bad. It was a one story, one room structure, made of boards, with a shingle roof. It had a well fitted door, and two glazed windows; and they papered the walls of the room with newspapers.—*By Miss Leslie.*

---

### CORRECTION.

In the receipt for Sponge Cake, No. 31., I omitted to mention the number of eggs to be used : put in ten.